Navigating Life

·

Foundations for Faith

Dave Phillips, D.Min.

Navigating Life

ISBN-13:   978-1483976778
ISBN-10:   1483976777

Printed in the United States of America

Navigating Life

DEDICATION

The inspiration to compile all these lessons into one book has come principally from my wife, Ann, who continues to encourage me in so many ways to become a dedicated worker in the field of ministry. Both of us have had the blessing of Christian parents who nurtured and sacrificed so that we might know the basic principles of Christianity. Although we were reared in different parts of the country, we shared remarkably similar experiences regarding our Christian walk. Ann's dedication as a Christian elementary-school teacher for over 25 years is second to none. Her labor of love has been a great blessing to our family, our children, and the hundreds of children she has taught. Doubtless, few of these children or parents fully appreciate her long days and nights of labor spent over lesson plans and papers. But as a dedicated husband, I thank her for her support in my relentless lifetime pursuit of knowledge and for daily encouragement to live for the Lord.

CONTENTS

PREFACE

It is a daunting task, if not impossible, to undertake an introduction to Christianity within the scope of one short book. The approach to any study must presuppose a familiarity with the topic on the part of the reader—or the study will be too basic to be of any benefit in conceptualizing the overall picture. Therefore, this book is intended as a 'launching point' for further reading to address the subject of Christianity.

Each of the topics introduced will at least indicate basic subjects that should be included in any discussion of Christianity regardless of the knowledge level of the reader. This basic review will be beneficial for the novice in the field as well as the mature Christian.

In order to engage in knowledgeable conversation regarding Christianity, one must be able to 'talk the talk.' Consequently, this book will provide a combined opportunity to learn Biblical terminology as well as theological concepts. As we survey the Bible content and become more familiar with the world of the Bible, we should understand that a full, in-depth survey of the Bible is not the goal of this book. The expressed goal is to begin the process of exploring the topic of Christianity as if it were being explained to someone interested in religion, aware of God, and motivated to learn all there is to know about Him.

1   TALKING THE TALK

·

An Introduction

I love baseball. But it is frustrating when the language used to describe the "all American game" has evolved so extensively over the years that it is a major challenge to keep up with the new lingo and participate in an active discussion with friends. When I was young, keeping track of runs, hits, and errors was sufficient for understanding what was happening in the game. Hitters had batting averages and pitchers had win-loss records that would define their status. Now, the statistics that describe performances are so intensely specific that the casual observer is left out of most conversations unless he remains current with the technical jargon. After all, whoever came up with the "slugging percentage" anyway?

Is this any different from most career paths? Mechanics, surgeons, stockbrokers, athletes, and educators all have their unique terms that challenge us. Who hasn't struggled with knowing exactly what the mechanic was trying to describe as being wrong with the car? Or hasn't the surgeon taken special precautions to translate the actual problems our loved ones have experienced following surgery?

I haven't even mentioned computer technology. Each industry and profession has its own career-specific language which either isolates specific thoughts with exacting language or variously facilitates or inhibits understanding and communication with the uninitiated.

The same dilemma faces religious topics. We can't communicate unless we have a shared meaning. And, sadly, many are discouraged from intense discussions regarding God because of their fear of using inappropriate language or not understanding specific descriptions. Not many are able to admit that they do not understand the basic terminology of such an important topic.

Why is understanding terminology so important? Because it is of no help to us to know the verbiage if the will of God is not understood. How can a person obey what he cannot understand? And if we are supposed to understand it, why do we allow the terminology to hinder us?

So we spend the time necessary to learn to "talk the talk." Not to impress, but to understand and communicate.

Basic Concepts

This book will explore, though not exhaustively define, ten individual concepts that are important to the believer. Fortunately, most believers will probably have already wrestled with each of these areas of study, but may have never thought about them together in this context.

You may even be surprised at how much you actually know about each concept, but have never had the opportunity to organize them in a systematic manner. But, knowing each of the following will help you "talk the talk," explore Biblical teachings, and formulate Christian practices in a more informed way

First of all, you should have a good understanding of **theology**. To which someone is bound to cry out, "Theology? I don't know anything about theology!" This would be quite an understatement, not to mention erroneous. *Theos*, the prefix of 'theology', is the Greek word for God. Since the suffix means "the study of", we have the understanding of theology as the study of God.

Now, just because you may not understand everything there is to know about God—who really does?—does not mean that you cannot be keenly interested in the subject. In fact, I would imagine that you already have some definite opinions about God. Some of these you have heard from significant people in your past, some you have developed as you have read the Bible or listened to religious teachers. Other beliefs you now hold have evolved from observations that you have made.

Can your conclusions stand the scrutiny of specific examination? In other words, can you defend your beliefs? This is why the study of God, theology, is so important. Looking back at the origin of our beliefs about God and questioning their integrity and truthfulness will not endanger our faith—it will build our faith.

Another word that is less common is **bibliology**. This word is defined as the study of the Scriptures. *Scripture* is a term that used to describe the written word of God, the inspired writings. We commonly think of the Bible as the Word of God, His inspired writings. But what do we really know about the Bible? Where did the Bible come from? How is it divided? To whom was it written? Who can interpret it?

These questions lead us back to a study of the book itself, a study that will help us find the roots of our belief. A proper understanding of the evolution of the book we call the Bible will prepare us to defend Biblical beliefs in spite of serious and intentional attacks against Christianity.

Christology is nothing more than the study of Jesus Christ, the son of God. Jesus Christ is understood to be the messiah spoken of so often in the Old Testament. The word messiah simply means savior. Since we tend to think of the name of Christ as a surname, it would be more accurate to name Jesus Christ as Jesus the Messiah. This term identifies Jesus as the fulfillment of the anointed savior.

The study of the life of Christ is crucial in our understanding of Christianity partly because there is so much misinformation about Jesus. Many historical works are labeled as biographies of Jesus when he was a child, but the content of these works is of human origin and determinedly unreliable. For example, the Gospel of Thomas purportedly details Jesus making a clay pigeon, turning it into a real pigeon, and then killing it. This, of course, is not only absent from the Bible, but an obvious significant change in character from any actions where miracles are so indiscriminate and pointless. One more recent author details the life of Jesus with imaginatively contrived episodes where Jesus interacts with others as a child and systematically learns of his divine, miraculous powers. So much misinformation can be, at the least, confusing and, at worst, deceiving.

A fourth important concept in correctly understanding Christianity is **pneumatology**, or the study of the Holy Spirit. The term "holy" simply means "set apart," so to refer to the Holy Spirit is to refer to the spirit of God.

This subject is probably the most challenging because so much is spoken of the Spirit and numerous eventualities are attributed to the Holy Spirit that most religious seekers are so confused they give up believing there is a pattern to the actions of the Spirit. On the other extreme, religious charlatans have made countless claims about the work of the Holy Spirit that some naïve religious seekers are led to believe that God actually informs certain preachers and teachers before he takes certain actions— thus giving them 'insight' unavailable to the rest of humanity. Fortunately, the Bible provides helpful insights into the work of the Spirit that prevents us from being deluded.

Anthropology, or the study of man, might seem an odd subject in discovering the essentials of Christianity. But, in reality, the study of man is necessary to understand the relationship between God and his created universe.

Our human origins do not have the definitive and documented explanation that the scientific world would have us believe. Many claims for authority in the scientific world are based on suppositions, which can often be questionable. A trip to the local museum or zoo will allow you to see what zoologists are teaching as the origin of man. Regardless of your training or belief, or even what you might hear or see in our public museums, zoos, and nature preservations, to say that the case for evolution has greatly overshadowed the case for creationism is a gross overstatement, In other words, don't believe all you've been told.

Teachers of science and history are constantly bombarded with pseudo-scientific research that is passed on as factual. But a review of their origins reveals the fallacies that are so casually overlooked in our science books. In our study, we simply explore where these concepts originated.

Hamartiology is the study of sin. The first part of the word comes from *hamartia*, the Greek word for sin. Sin needs to be defined from a biblical perspective and traced down through the history of man, as recorded in the Bible. Our study of sin will not be a categorization of various types of sins with detailed explanations, but rather a look at ways in which man has failed to live up to the expectations of God. The process of falling into sin is progressive and systematic. But, thankfully, God has provided a complete explanation in the Bible which equips us to be successfully victorious over its power and ultimate consequence.

Soteriology is the sixth key word. It is simply defined as the study of salvation. Along with the explanation of sin, God has revealed the means by which a person may be saved.

A novice will say "saved from what?" This is an excellent question.

One who has little or no knowledge of the Bible will have difficulty understanding that there are consequences for our actions. We may hear leaders in society speak of heaven and hell, but may never really have had any serious, thoughtful considerations about the realities of both places.

Because of the changing nature of religious groups and the growing trend of world religions in heretofore Christian environments, beliefs regarding the afterlife vary dramatically. Because of the lack of acceptance of the Bible as authoritative by many of these groups, it is becoming increasingly less likely that the Bible will be used in our conclusions. So, this discussion is greatly needed.

Angelology is the study of angels, demons, and Satan. It isn't uncommon to hear most people speak of their belief in these three spiritual realities—but what isn't as clear is our belief about their individual origin and characteristics.

Many believe that when we die we will become angels. Is that what we will eventually become?

Others believe that demons still overpower an individual and "take control" of his or her body so that certain actions are unavoidable. Demon possession—does this still happen today?

Others describe a cosmic battle between two super-powers—Jesus and Satan. Jesus narrowly wins and thus Satan is consigned to imprisonment, awaiting cosmic destruction. Is this what Christians believe?

This topic will challenge your ability not only to describe your belief, but to defend it.

Ecclesiology is the study of the church. The first part of the word in Greek (*ekklesia*) means "the called out." Those who answer the call of Jesus Christ are called into a spiritual body that is termed the church. Since our understanding of soteriology necessarily implies that there is a group of "saved" people, we now look at how this unique body of believers lives and acts, both as individuals and as a group.

The last topic we will explore is that of **eschatology**. The word comes from the Greek word *eskaton*, which means "last things." This is a very important topic because our understanding of our ultimate destiny will help formulate our plan for present-day living and motivate us to greater service.

Again, conflicting theories of the afterlife will confuse us if we are not careful, so we will want to explore what the Bible says in various places about the life which is to come.

Talking Points

I began by saying that the game of baseball continues to evolve, though the basic concept of the game remains the same. We now view it from a different perspective. When I learn to coach my son or daughter's T-ball team and carefully demonstrate the proper method of hitting the ball and running the base paths, I don't claim to be an expert manager. I may not be able to explain the pitching strategies of a major league pitcher or the nuances of a pick-off play, but I am now opening the door for further development—planting the seed that will later be cultivated and watered for growth. And that is exciting.

Just that I now know the categories of a basic study in Christianity does not make me a Biblical scholar. But, these are the very pathways that must be traversed by every Biblical scholar, so we are at least on the right road. Our goal is to know the identity of Jesus Christ and know the magnitude of his love for each soul, a love that lead to an extreme sacrifice on a hastily erected cross in full view of a mocking, relentless crowd of mistaken religious zealots. This sacrifice is the focal point of all Scripture, and the reason for our eternal hope.

Though we will understandably not exhaust full understanding of these ten themes, they do, however, at least introduce the novice and remind the veteran of the importance of knowing what God has already stated, and impress all believers even more deeply with the work of God. Our discussion will provide the framework for your "talking the talk" of Christianity and motivate us all in our "walking the walk" of our Lord and savior Jesus Christ.

Chapter 1 · *What You Should Know...*

Theology · the study of God

Bibliology · the study of the Scriptures

Christology · the study of Christ

Pneumatology · the study of the Spirit

Anthropology · the study of man

Hamartiology · the study of sin

Soteriology · the study of salvation

Angelology · the study of angels

Ecclesiology · the study of the church

Eschatology · study of last things

Dave Phillips

.

2   THE STUDY OF GOD

Theology

A *theologian*. Sounds stilted, doesn't it? Stuffy…stiff…perhaps 'snooty?'

Your mind quickly draws a mental picture of a bearded man, wire rim glasses in one hand, deep in thought, leaning back in his rocker with eyes glassily gazing toward the sky, stroking his chin with the thumb and forefinger of his other hand. Occasionally, he mutters an indiscernible groan, as if he just came upon a novel thought casting never-before-discovered light upon current conditions. What a stroke of genius!

You might think, "Well, that's just not me, if that's what it takes to discuss God." But wait just a minute.

That may be a stereotype of a theologian, but that does not make it reality. We have mental images of several activities that are based on hearsay and not fact. Not all athletes are muscular nor are all actresses beautiful. The best teachers are not always in a classroom and perhaps the best cooks are not professional chefs.

Here is an interesting thought. Everyone that has thought seriously about God, perhaps to the point of researching the topic, is a theologian. This probably includes you.

Breaking a word down helps, so let's begin with a simple definition of theology. *Theos* means "God," and *logia* means, "oracles, words, and messages." Theology is nothing more than the study of God. For that reason, anyone who studies God or reflects on the existence or purpose of the Creator of the universe, by definition, participates in the practice of theology.

Actually, it's a very important task. Arguably it is *the* most important task. The importance of considering God is seen when you recognize questions that many have asked. For example, an elementary student listens to the guide at the museum discuss the proposed evolutionary progression of man…only she doesn't mention the word 'proposed.'

The student begins wondering about how the universe originated. Where and when did life begin? Or maybe he wonders if the guide is correct in determining the age of the earth. How can we know for sure? The question is whether we can actually tell how old the earth actually is. Can it be conclusively proven that the universe is billions of years old? Even if the age of the physical earth could be proven, could we postulate that the world was created to *appear* billions of years old?

Then, we face the questions regarding evil. If God created the world, where did evil come from? Where did Satan come from? Why didn't (or doesn't) God just annihilate Satan, if He is so much more powerful?

If God is so good, why do people suffer? Why do babies die? Or why do innocent, dutiful, faithful mothers contract deadly diseases? Does God care?

Speaking of God, does he care about *me* and *my* problems? Am I considered unique in his sight, or am I just another created being like all the other mammals? And if there is a God, how am I supposed to know what He wants me to do? With such a variety of religions, who is right? Or is *anyone* actually *right*?

And there are more questions, questions regarding your future, questions about decisions you make every day at work, questions about the afterlife. Maybe you have even wondered if there really is life after death. Maybe you've had questions about Jesus and his relationship with God.

You see, you probably have wrestled with some, if not all, of these questions at some point in your life. And you have probably come to some conclusions…maybe several conclusions. Likely, you have changed your mind on several of your conclusions over the course of time. Your answers to these vital questions may depend on what time of the year it is, or on what kind of difficulties you are currently facing. It's natural to change our minds from time to time while thinking about such issues. But theology is a serious discipline that has to do with the foundational concepts that guide our decisions, our activities, and ultimately, our destiny.

The Sources of Theology

Since theology is so important, we must pay close attention to where we go for our information. The source for our information may be more important than the information itself. If the source is unreliable, then the conclusions may be undependable. Even if the conclusion was accurate, how would you defend it?

You may have thought that the search for truth is a relatively recent pursuit. I don't really know exactly why we think of ourselves to be so much more clever and intelligent than our forefathers. But, the search for truth is not unique to the twenty-first century. Philosophers have been wrestling with the concept of truth and eternity for centuries.

There is a difference, however, between a casual search for the truth about life and our religion. The difference is that religion not only purports to have the "truth" about the future of man, but also the way in which he "should live" while here on earth. If there is an eternal purpose that God has for man, we are involved in a study with eternal consequences.

If there is a certain truth that exists from God about man's purpose, then our search takes on a greater sense of urgency and our indefensible claims about truth become just personal opinions. If there is an eternal truth, the pressing of our personal opinions on others becomes inexcusable.

We do know there are two kinds of truth. Absolute truth is truth that exists apart from the individual. The individual may or may not be aware of its existence, but certainly it does not alter the facts of its existence. Many people at one time honestly believed that the earth was flat, but the earth was, and still is, round. Many cultures believe in evil spirits that inhabit a body, bringing with it sickness and diseases. Others believe that the gods who are unhappy with our conduct will cause us to be sick. Modern medicine has taught us that germs and viruses cause disease.

Relative truth is nothing more than subjective truth—truth that differs according to each individual, according to his tastes and preference. If I like peanut butter, it is a relative truth that peanut butter is good. If, however, I am allergic to peanuts, peanut butter would not be good for me.

Spiritual truth is thought by many to be subjective rather than objective.

This means that spiritual truth is thought to be different for one person than it is for another and one can never really know the truth for sure. You will hear it voiced with statements like, "I believe in my faith and my God, you believe in yours." Or, "You worship God the way you desire, and I'll worship Him in my way. Neither one of us is wrong."

If this is accurate, then why would anyone be concerned about converting anyone? Why not just allow everyone to live the way they want to live and leave them along. Interestingly, this is exactly what many believe and teach.

But, suppose there is one absolute, spiritual truth. Suppose that God had one plan for mankind and we are responsible for living according to His plan in order to be blessed eternally. Would that change your attitude toward spiritual truth?

Think about it for a moment. If there is only one God, would He try to confuse us by sending contradictory messages about himself? What purpose would be served by confusing man about the God of the universe?

Since there are so many views about God, where did each originate? Why would man be so confused? Could it be that we have taken our subjective truth (our feelings, opinions, and personal beliefs) and adopted them as absolute truth? Wouldn't it be true that if we cannot substantiate our beliefs in some authoritative way, then we must accept them only as personal opinions? So we come to the search for truth.

Does God Exist?

This question is basic to our interest in studying Christianity. If God does not exist, then all the concern about serving Jesus is nothing but an extremely cruel hoax. If there is no reason to believe that Jesus is the son of God or that Jesus is the means by which man can receive divine blessings and eternal life, then we are wasting our time in delusional thinking. If there is no God, is there any reason to believe there is life after death?

After all, a skeptic (one who believes that the existence of God cannot be proven) claims there is no evidence or proof that God exists, much less that He created the world. If a supposed God is in existence, He certainly has not made any attempt to prove his existence. Additionally, the arguments that believers make concerning his existence are all based on theories, stories, or myths. Forms of these myths are evident in every society and represent and could be explained as the result of creative minds that sought to pass down generational beliefs and customs.

However, that supposition brings us to the ultimate challenging question. If there is no God that had the power to create the world, how did the world come into existence? The ultimate evidence proving the necessity of a Creator would be that the earth does exist. It is a physical, animate object that could not just have suddenly appeared without some kind of beginning point.

Three Possibilities for Creation

There are three possibilities regarding the creation of the universe. First, there is the explanation offered by many scientists which states that the world simply evolved from a reforming of matter that existed, possibly including a cosmic explosion (the big bang) resulting in the forming of the sun, moon, stars, etc. A popular argument, called adaptation theory, postulates that simple organisms evolved from a lower form to a higher form based on the need for survival in a new environment. Therefore, animals and man have been able to survive only when they are able to physically adapt to meet the needs of the changing society. In 1859, Charles Darwin, one of the leading proponents of this theory, called it 'survival of the fittest' in his monumental work, *Origin of Species*. This process of evolution has been accepted and taught in many schools, libraries, museums, public zoos, and national parks to the point that many children simply assume that it is true. Many have not heard any critiques.

But the evolutionist must be able to respond to several issues that arise. For example, the process of evolution does not provide evidence for a belief in an eternal series, that is, where life is passed on from generation to

generation. If there is an evolution, what is the ultimate source from which life evolved? If that source can be determined, then we are able to begin discussion of incremental, necessary changes.

A second issue is that evolution contains no link or connection that demonstrates these lower orders of being actually evolving into a higher level. We have no evidence of dead matter suddenly becoming alive. There is no evidence of animals actually becoming human. This common picture supposedly demonstrates the evolution of man.

But when charts like these which are used to show the evolution of man from monkeys are actually critically reviewed, the diagrams prove not only to be deceiving in the order of their occurrence (the time frames of their findings do not prove a progression) and the drawings showing the actual monkey is the product of a scientist's theory as to how the monkey might look.

For example, taking one bone supposed to be from a leg and deducing what the jawbone and skull would look like using the same dimensions is more a representation of calculated creativity on the part of the scientist rather than demonstrable science.

Additionally, if there is an evolution from monkey to man—or a transition from fish to an amphibian to a mammal—it seems fair to ask the evolutionist to produce evidence of creatures that are currently in the midst of the process. Many claim that a 'split' occurred at one point in time where some animals began the evolutionary process, while others remained within their own species. But the reason for this sudden, not as yet repeated, life-altering change needs to be given. As of yet, there is no explanation.

Bill Nye, *The Science Guy*, states on his website, Anomic Office Drone, "If you want to deny evolution and live in your world, in your world that's completely inconsistent with everything we observe in the universe, that's fine, but don't make your kids do it because we need them. We need scientifically literate voters and taxpayers for the future." What Nye does not offer is an alternative explanation. He assumes that science has answered all the questions and that science offers no mystery. However, science cannot document or even identify origins. Where did man originate? Where did the first man live? Science can only study with empirical evidence (research based on experience or observation of evidence) and cannot explain sources.

The second of three conclusions regarding the origin of the universe is that of creation, or as termed in our society, intelligent design. There are many thoughts concerning the Creator that brought the world into existence, but most would agree that the Biblical record regarding the creation sufficiently explains it.

The creationist must admit that scientific evidence regarding the creation of the world cannot be fully demonstrated. As the Bible records, the belief is based on faith. But it should also quickly be added that the basis for faith is complete to those who will observe and consider the evidence.

The world and the created orders are a convincing warrant for faith in a supreme Creator. This conclusion is not evidence for the God of the Bible, but rather for faith in the fact that some higher order created the world. The existence of this world is the primary witness. There are heavens, firmament, and harmony among the creation. Several specific arguments will be offered later, but the fact that we live on a planet that exists among an ordered creation provides the basis for belief that it was designed by someone or something of an understandably complex nature.

The third conclusion regarding the origin of the universe is that of agnosticism or skepticism. An atheist is one who believes there is no God. An agnostic believes that you cannot know if there is a God unless you are told. With no individual being directly addressed by the Creator, the logical conclusion is that the issue will remain a mystery.

While the conclusion of the agnostic may at first sound like a safe alternative, it contains two less than desirable potential consequences. The first consequence is that if the Bible is true, then we have been told and are expected to respect the desires of the Creator as revealed in the revelation. The Bible describes tremendous blessings for those faithful to the Word and severe consequences to those who disobey, or, in this case, to those who do not believe.

The second consequence is that at first glance the agnostic position seems to be the more humble position, since it assumes nothing that is not obvious. However, agnostics believe that you cannot know—a position that is more dogmatic about the certainty that nothing can be known about the universe. In fact, an agnostic would argue that you cannot know anything for sure—a statement that in itself is contradictory. How can one know that he cannot know?

The Atheist's Great Dilemma

Dinesh D'Souza, author of *What's So Great About Christianity?* has regularly debated skeptics and says, "Atheism has taken a militant attack against Christianity. This is odd if they are being led by evidence. Why so angry? Why care? I don't believe in unicorns, but I don't write about it."

Antony Flew, a prolific atheist for most of his life, says in his book, *There is a God*, that the world of atheism maintains modern science is based on three great assumptions. These are: (a) nature obeys laws, (b) recognition of the intelligently organized and purpose-driven beings which arose from matter, and (c) the existence of nature. After a lifetime of teaching there is no God, he changed his view in later years and admitted that the world "was brought into existence by an infinite intelligence."

Given the existence of life, the atheist cannot explain (a) the origin of life, (b) the origin of consciousness, and (c) the origin of morality. In determining right or wrong, the atheist would say right or wrong for humans is based on selfishness. Yet, there is no explanation for a sense of selfless love or altruism so prevalent among mankind.

It is time for us to look at the formal arguments for God that have been handed down through the generations that argue there is no rational explanation of the world, nor of man, nor of personality, without the existence of a living God.

Commonplace Proofs for God

The proofs for God could be summarized very simply and with less complexity. It might be these three proofs are sufficient for those of us wanting to know the basic principles of the Bible. I offer these first before I give the more abstract theories held by philosophers, theologians and believers over the years. You may not need or desire to explore these theories. However, you may be talking to children or grandchildren that may ask you specific questions as they wrestle with their faith. It is in the spirit of being able to defend the faith and answer challenging queries that I offer these thoughts.

The first proof for believing in God is life itself. It may be unexplainable but it is undeniable. We are here and we are full of life. Though we may not know the means by which the life came to be in the cells, we know it did because we see it.

The second proof is the existence of law or of certainties which we have defined as laws. There are, for example, the laws of gravity, atrophy, etc. If there is a law, there must be a will because law is the expression of the will of the one giving the law.

The third proof is the existence of love. Self-preservation is characteristic of most animals and yet humans are sacrificial in their expressions of love. Love is the master passion of the world—unexplainable without a sense of specific purpose given to them.

Historically, there have been numerous formal arguments making the case for the existence of God. H. Wayne House has summarized many of them in his book, *Charts of Christian Theology and Doctrine* (Zondervan, 1992). I believe it can be accurately summarized that most of these arguments will be based upon recognizing a present experience or observation—and reasoning back to where the source of that action might have originated. For example, people have observed motion and concluded that something must have caused it—for nothing moves on its own initiative. Or a person might observe that everyone desires truth, so there must be something that is perfectly true. These arguments can be quite complex and confusing. However, the following list of the five most historically popular arguments are summarized so that you may be aware of the thought behind the conclusion

Five Popular Formalized Arguments
For the Existence of God

The Argument from Intuition

Augustine, from the 4th and 5th centuries A.D., believed from his own feelings and from his observations that man has a direct intuition of the existence of God. There is something about human beings that cause them to know that we and the universe are products of God.

In fact, ancient peoples have historically had conceptions of a 'future life.' The Greeks believed in the Elysium (fields or plains), the resting place of the heroic. The Teutons (of Germanic or Celtic origin) believed in Valhalla (hall of the slain), which was a home for those who were gloriously slain in battle. The Hebrews believed in paradise. The American Indian believed in the happy hunting ground.

The Ontological Argument

This is a metaphysical argument (the word ontology comes from the word *ontos*, which is defined as "of being"). A Christian philosopher and theologian of the eleventh century by the name of Anselm posed that "God is that than which nothing greater can be conceived." He said that if we could conceive of a God that could exist, then there is an *idea* of God. Some argued that you could make up a fictitious god—but Anselm would reply that your fictitious god is not as great as the greatest conceivable God, because he (the fictitious god) does not exist.

Anselm would continue, "But I can think of something that is *greater than the idea* of that than which there is no greater." You ask, "What would that be?" He would say, "It is the *existence* of that than which is no greater." He concludes, "So, by definition, God must exist."

Anselm's arguments represent the most complex of the formalized arguments for the existence of God. You need not accept it. But you need to be aware of the existence of the argument.

The Moral Argument

Immanuel Kant discussed a "sense of ought," a moral sense within man is an innate capacity to know right and wrong. That man has this capacity can hardly be explained unless there is a moral governor of the universe. It implies a moral Creator, God.

One of the better known authors whose work represents that of the moral argument is C.S. Lewis. Lewis argues that when children are playing games together, they automatically begin to argue that someone acted unfairly or wrong in the way they treated them. Lewis purports that this sense of fairness is something that is innate within each of us. Regardless of whether we believe there is a God, we know that there is some moral governor of the universe that has given us standards by which to live.

The Cosmological Argument

Thomas Aquinas (late middle ages) is credited with the classical statement of the cosmological argument—"the existing cosmos is an undeniable evidence of a Creator." He said that everything must have some antecedent cause. There is a need for (a) an unmoved mover—prime mover, (b) an uncaused first cause, and (c) a necessary being.

A frequently used illustration is the demonstration of a billiard ball suddenly beginning to move across a billiard table. Something had to cause the ball to move. Whatever caused the ball to move had to have something else that caused it to move... and so on. For every movement there is some cause. Tracing all the way back to the initial cause is to trace your way back to God.

The Teleological Argument

Thomas Aquinas is also given credit with the classical statement of the teleological argument—"the universe demonstrates order and design, hence there must be a designer."

The word teleological comes from the Greek word, *telos*, which means "end or purpose." The existence of order and system demands an orderer. Beauty, form, design, and purpose in nature all imply a creative mind, an intelligent architect. In addition, the gradations of being, which are all about us, require that which has the quality in the superlative degree. The existence of something, or some quality, implies the absolute. Therefore, an orderly universe implies a perfect source from which the universe has come. You look at the end result and infer there was an originator.

These five classical arguments are not the only arguments, nor are they necessarily original with the individuals listed. But these individuals have historically been identified as people who gave a voice to these positions. There are numerous other arguments offered, but none has received near as much acceptance or promotion as the five listed above.

Chapter 2 · *What You Should Know...*

· why we could all be considered theologians

· difference between absolute and subjective truth

· three possibilities for explaining the existence of the world

· three commonplace proofs for the existence of God

· five classical arguments for the existence of God.

3   THE STUDY OF SCRIPTURES

Bibliology

The word "Bible" comes from a Greek word *biblia*, the plural form of the word *biblion*. It means book or record. The term *Bible* can be somewhat misleading if you think of it as one book. Many people will say "I've read through the Bible" as if they have read a novel or history book. If you've ever tried to read through the Bible and become discouraged and quit, there may be a very good reason. The Bible is not one book, but can rather be more properly identified as a library of books. Each book in the Bible has a different purpose, and in fact has a different theme.

And here is the reason why it is important to understand the various themes. Some individuals have heard of the value of reading the Bible and so they purchase one with all the intentions of reading it through to the end to get a big picture of the message. Obviously, you start at the beginning, so they dive into reading Genesis, and it is an excellent read. There are stories, descriptions, adventures, consequences, and histories of people.

Encouraged, they launch into Exodus and it, too, is a good read. Moses is leading the Israelites out of Egyptian bondage, and since the name of Moses is so well known, and the story has plenty of intrigue, the reader is excited. He lays down the book, excited to pick it up again at the next sitting.

But then we face Leviticus. The new reader begins reading with high expectations, only to find a seemingly endless list of laws and details that confuse rather than clarify. The rules, laws, and commandments seem so disjointed, that the weary reader finally lays the book down, ready to tackle it on another day, only to find that 'another day' just never comes.

Some determine that perhaps the best place to begin might not be the Old Testament, so they turn to the book of Matthew and begin reading in the New Testament. Only Matthew begins by going through a frustrating list of genealogies, with names that no one uses anymore, and the reader throws his proverbial hands up in despair and lays the book aside.

Unfortunately, this is one of the reasons we don't know the Bible. We haven't read the text, and the reason we haven't read the text is that we didn't have an introduction to the nature of the book. So, let me suggest another approach.

In order to fully appreciate each book of the Bible and view it in its proper perspective, I would like to emphasize a much broader view of Bible history. Perhaps the following overly-simplistic chart will help one's understanding, especially when coupled with a brief explanation.

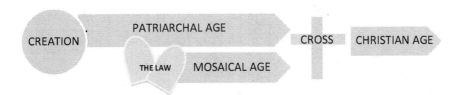

The chart begins with the creation of the world, in which God created substance, hills, rocks, valleys, and oceans, out of nothing. The Bible says He *spoke* it into existence. This explanation assumes that the reader believes that the Biblical explanation for the origin of all things is correct. When God spoke, physical objects came into existence that were not in existence before. The actual process of these objects appearing is shrouded in mystery, but the fact that something was created is evidenced by their existence in the present day.

When God spoke the world into existence, He culminated his creation on the sixth day with the creation of man and woman. God had created a world (universe) where man, animals, birds and mammals could live.

The chart shows various spans of time that are not explicitly defined in the Bible. For example, you will not read of the 'patriarchal age' in so many words, but the concept and practice can be traced throughout the first part of the Old Testament. The word patriarchal is made up of *patros*, which is the Greek word for father, and *arche*, which is the Greek word for rule. It describes the fact that God spoke with the fathers in the beginning of time and anticipated their leading their individual families. God spoke to Adam and Eve, but it was Adam who was held primarily responsible for the sin because he listened to the voice of his wife. The implication was that he knew what God's will was and was to be held accountable for his actions.

God spoke to Abraham, the great patriarch, in Genesis 12, and his family was to follow his lead. Abraham's son Isaac and his grandson Jacob (Israel) were known as patriarchs because they were the leaders of their family. In honoring their father, the family found favor with God. This was held to be the norm for all families regardless of their lineage.

During the time of Moses, however, God chose to deliver a special set of commandments to the children of Israel. What we now know as the first five books of the Old Testament were given specifically to the Jews, that is, the descendants of Abraham through Isaac. Since the promise of God was to bless all of mankind through the descendant of Abraham (specifically named as Isaac in Genesis 17:19), the law was given that the people would come to know how God interacts with those that follow him. In fact, the Old Testament is called a "schoolmaster," or tutor, that leads one to Christ (Gal. 3:24). The Jewish people were to be the model of those that would learn how to interact with God in a way that would be acceptable.

Please notice this important point. The books of Law (the Pentateuch, or torah) were given only to Jews. Those who were not Jewish were not held accountable to the Old Law. They could, if they so chose, determine to follow the Old Law. If so, they were to be known as proselytes, another name for a convert. But they would retain their heritage and be known as Gentiles, even though they were practicing the Jewish faith.

In other words, if someone were to ask me today whether I keep the commandments of the Old Testament, I would respond that I do not. That might sound strange to many religious people, even some Christians, but it need not alarm anyone. I am not Jewish, and because of that, I would never have been amenable to the Old Testament. I would have been living as a Gentile, answerable to the patriarchal system of living obediently to the laws of the fathers and the land in which I lived.

In the New Testament, we read that the place of the Old Testament was as a tutor to lead us to Christ. Now that Jesus has come in the flesh and successfully demonstrated his victory over death, we are now living under a covenant that is based on the sacrifice of Jesus rather than the sacrificial system of the Old Testament. The Old Testament has a new place in the historical work of Jesus. It hasn't been destroyed. Jesus said, however, that it has been fulfilled. In the Sermon on the Mount, Jesus clearly states that his purpose for coming to the earth was that the Old Law would be fulfilled. We now see the purposes of God unfold in the Old Testament and consummated in the New Testament.

Some eager Christians profess to be faithful to the Old Testament and the New Testament. But the Old Testament was written to instruct Jews with the added promise that in time the blessings of God would rest also on Gentiles (Gal. 3:8). The sacrificial system of the Old Testament was insufficient for the forgiveness of sins (Heb. 10:1ff.), while the blood of Jesus Christ, fully described in the New Testament, *is* able to meet the divine conditions for forgiveness of sins.

You will notice on the chart that there are several divisions of books in the Old Testament as well as the New Testament. It is very helpful to our understanding of God's plan for mankind to have an adequate memory device for knowing the themes of each of the books. There are several that are helpful. Each of them will be similar to the following list of books and an appropriate phrase to help us remember their themes.

Genesis · Story of the creation of the world, the fall of man, the flood, and the origins of families.

Exodus · Details God's leading the Israelites out of Egyptian bondage by empowering the great leader Moses.

Leviticus · Instructions for specific offerings and feasts required by God which set an example for understanding the sacrifice of Christ.

Numbers · Israelites wandering in the wilderness.

Deuteronomy · A series of sermons in which Moses recalls how God deals with his people.

Joshua · Joshua leads the Israelites in conquering and claiming the Promised Land.

Judges · God's response and rescue of the wayward Israelites.

Ruth · A love story in the midst of adversity.

1 Samuel · Saul's disastrous reign as king and his attacks on David.

2 Samuel · David's reign as king, including successes and failures.

1 Kings · Solomon's reign and eventual sin, setting the stage for the division of the kingdom.

2 Kings · Israel and Judah continue to sin, resulting in exile.

1 Chronicles · A look at God's faithfulness from Adam to David.

2 Chronicles · A focus on Judah, David's descendants, and concern for the temple and its worship.

Ezra · Return from captivity to build the temple and rededicate the people.

Nehemiah · Rebuilding the wall around Jerusalem.

Esther · The Queen of Persia is used to spare Israel from extermination.

Job · The problem of suffering and man's response.

Psalms · The songs and prayers of the Jews.

Proverbs · Wisdom of Solomon.

Ecclesiastes · Vanity of earthly pursuits and reminder of heavenly perspective.

Song of Solomon · Glorification of love in marriage.

Isaiah · The Messianic prophet—the punishment and promises of God to Israel.

Jeremiah · A message to the city of Jerusalem regarding impending doom.

Lamentations · A funeral dirge for the city of Jerusalem and God's people.

Ezekiel · Message to exiles regarding the power of God.

Daniel · Dreams of Daniel and prophecies regarding the coming kingdom.

Hosea · Message to the Northern Kingdom condemning their unfaithfulness and expressing God's desire for restoration.

Joel · A locust plague becomes an occasion to call the Jews to repentance and tells of the events surrounding the glorious future for God's people.

Amos · A herdsman who charges God's people with sin and calls them back from self-serving worship to sacrificial dedication to God.

Obadiah · Because of their lack of assistance and arrogance when Judah (Jacob's descendants) was plundered, Obadiah pronounces judgment on Edom (descendants of Esau).

Jonah · The reluctant preacher is sent to Nineveh with a message of deliverance.

Micah · Micah prophesies to both Israel and Judah, outlining God's rebuke of the people and his expectations for their behavior.

Nahum · Prophecy of the destruction of Nineveh because of its rejection of God.

Habakkuk · Prophet questions God and is told to have faith in a sovereign God.

Zephaniah · Prophecy of Babylon taking Judah into captivity.

Haggai · Prophet sent to stir up Jews to complete the building of the temple in Jerusalem.

Zechariah · Highly figurative prophecy concerning God's rule over the people and His ultimate vindication of God's people.

Malachi · A prophetic dialogue concerning the progression of sin and the need for faithfulness.

Matthew · Probably written primarily to Jews and appealing to the Scriptures, Matthew describes Jesus as the Messiah, the king of the Jews.

Mark · Probably written to non-Jews (because of explanations of Jewish customs) and calling attention to the miracles, Mark describes Jesus' role as servant of man.

Luke · Written to Theophilus and representing an appeal to the thoughtful and cultured mind, Luke describes Jesus as the ideal, universal man.

John · The last of the Gospel writers, John specifically states his intent is to show that Jesus is the Son of God (John 20:30, 31).

Acts · The beginning and the formation of the church.

Romans · Paul's description of the work of Christ in the lives of Christians.

1 Corinthians · Paul's correspondence to Corinth discusses problems in the church.

2 Corinthians · Paul defends his apostleship and opens his heart to the struggling church.

Galatians · Paul's response to Christians tempted to go back to the Law.

Ephesians · Paul writes about the teachings of the church and the duties of the Christian.

Philippians · One of four prison epistles, Paul writes a letter of encouragement from a Roman confinement.

Colossians · One of four prison epistles, Paul focuses on Christ's deity.

1 Thessalonians · Paul encourages a young church to keep focused on serving God.

2 Thessalonians · Paul again writes the young church to continue working while waiting for the Lord to come.

1 Timothy · Paul gives instructions on caring for the church.

2 Timothy · Paul emphasizes the need to learn, practice and preach the Word of God.

Titus · Paul details a conduct manual for the church.

Philemon · One of four prison epistles, Paul explains the transformation of a runaway slave to a brother in Christ.

Hebrews · Message to a discouraged church about the glorious Messiah who has ushered in a new covenant.

James · Message to build and bolster one's faith in God.

1 Peter · Letter to a persecuted church offering comfort and encouragement.

2 Peter · Warning to a church about potential false teachers and the possibility of apostasy.

1 John · Letter that emphasizes the love of Christ and the need for Christian fellowship.

2 John · Caution against false teachers.

3 John · John gives instruction on handling those who are arrogant and self-serving.

Jude · Jude writes for the need to contend for the faith.

Revelation · Dramatic story of the ultimate victory of Christ.

How the Bible Is Divided—and
What We Should Know

Since there are so many different ideas about the Bible, it should come as no surprise to us that not everyone has the same idea about the Bible as we do. In fact, there are some religious groups that do not believe the Bible is even necessary in order to worship and serve God. One graduate student in a doctoral program at a state university was also a preacher for a certain religious group. In one of our sessions, he told me that a person does not even need the Bible to learn about Jesus Christ. I was amazed at his comment since we would not know about Jesus were it not for the words of the Bible. But his beliefs were admittedly not dependent on the Bible.

There are individuals, many of them very devout in their practice and sincere in their diligence, who have misconceptions about the Bible.

Whether it is because of the way in which certain passages of the Bible have been taught in times past or the way in which the teachings of the Bible have been scorned by those that are close to them, there is a need for clarification on the structure, purpose and benefit of the Bible.

For example, the Bible is a collection of books. Many are historical in nature, others are poetic, several are narratives, while others are letters written to various recipients. Some of the recipients of these letters are individuals, some are churches, while still others are groups of various nationalities (Jews and/or Gentiles). Understanding the author of the book and the intended audience is crucial to understanding the meaning. If I am to understand the meaning for my life, I must first know the original meaning to the initial audience.

Whatever the nature of the text, (historical, narrative, prophecy, etc.) each part of the Bible has been divided into chapters and verses. These were not in the original text, and as such, are not inspired by God. The first attempt to divide the Scriptures is attributed to a catholic cardinal (Hugo de Sancto Caro), who was creating a concordance of the Latin Vulgate. The Vulgate is a Latin translation of the Bible made by a 4th century priest named Jerome. The division of the chapters was made so that individual parts of the Scriptures might be notated and referenced for study. But, the divisions that have been passed down to us are most likely those of Stephen Langton, an English churchman, in the year 1227. They were used in the Wycliffe English Bible, which was circulated in 1382.

The chapters were subsequently divided into verses by a Jewish teacher, Mordecai Nathan, in 1448. Since the year 1560, when the Geneva Bible was published in Paris, almost all Bibles published have used a later system developed by Robert Estienne (Stephanus).

This is important to know because we may feel like one chapter represents the end of a complete thought much like an author might design a novel or classroom textbook. But, frequently the thoughts of an entire text can cross chapter lines (and separation of verses) to form a part of a whole thought on an intended topic. In other words, we should not assume that when we come to the end of Acts 1, that the author has changed topics and settings for the beginning of Acts 2. In John 13, Jesus is having a supper with his apostles that lasts the entirety of John chapters 14-16.

In addition, you should know that paragraph headings are inserted into many translations that signal the topic for the following passage. These are frequently very helpful in dividing lines of thought. But they, too, are added by a translator and are not a part of the inspired text. They are often helpful, but can sometimes be misleading. Just remember which part is inspired (the text) and which is an addition (the sometimes opinionated addition). No need to find a Bible with no textual helps—just remember the difference.

One other precaution you should remember is that when scholars are translating words, they frequently insert words that will help the reader understand the meaning and make the reading smoother. These words that are inserted are always italicized. In modern reading, we generally use italics to emphasize the word. We generally give greater prominence when reading the text aloud. For example, the King James Version translates 2 Corinthians 6:14, "Be ye not unequally yoked together with unbelievers." In the original Greek language, the word *'unequally'* does not appear. The translators, however, were trying to get across the concept that a mismatch between two people is indicated and the word 'unequally' is used. The New American Standard Version translates the same verse, "Do not be bound together with unbelievers." But the word translated 'bound together' literally means to 'be mismated.' The only point that we should remember is that when reading the Bible, the italicized words are not intended to be emphasized but rather designed to be helpful.

Which Translation of the Bible Should I Use?

Many individuals spend many years and a great deal of expense to discuss this very important topic. Since this is an introduction to Christianity and not an in-depth analysis of biblical scholarship, I would like to make several basic points.

First of all, the best place to begin in Bible study is with any Bible that you will read. If a person will not read the Bible, it really doesn't make much difference which translation it is. There are many good translations—and it seems there are more coming out all the time. I don't believe that it is a dishonest attempt to sell more Bibles. I believe that people are genuinely wrestling with the Scriptures—which is a good thing.

Second, you should make sure that you get a translation and not a paraphrase. A translation is an interpretation by scholars who are translating ancient texts on a word-for-word basis. They ask questions like, "What did this Hebrew word mean at the time it was written?" "How has this Greek word changed in meanings over the years?" The idea is to present as close to an accurate translation of the original text as is possible.

A paraphrase, however, is an attempt to translate the meaning of the ancient text—not necessarily word for word but rather concept by concept—in language that is more contemporary. Frequently, however, those that paraphrase texts change the meaning of the text and it loses some of its specific significance to those that desire to follow Christ. The changes can frequently be subtle but still misleading.

So, do I have to study Hebrew and Greek to understand the Bible? I like what Neale Pryor, a Hebrew scholar and Bible professor at Harding University, once said when asked what the passage said in the original language. He said, "Pretty much what it says in the English." His advice was to get several good translations (not paraphrases) and compare them to determine what the New Testament says to us today. I think that is good advice.

Third, you should get a translation that you can read and understand. The King James Version is written on a 12th grade reading level. It doesn't mean that it cannot be understood. It does mean that in most churches we will have to stop and explain the wording in order to understand it. The New International Version is written on a seventh grade reading level. When our children were young, I bought them each a New International Version of the Bible so that they could read with understanding. Then, as issues would arise, we could talk about what the Bible says. As I remember, we didn't have many in-depth discussions of issues. But, I did see that they carried, read and used their Bibles when we would attend church services.

The New American Standard Bible is the one I use and from which I preach. It is written on an 11th grade reading level and is as close to the original languages as any I have found. When I prepare to preach, I double-check the words in the verses I will preach from, and have generally found that the words in the original text are the words that are in this version. This translation has been accused of not being as 'smooth' as the King James Version nor as easy to understand as the New International Version, but I have found that if I study the correct words, I can get the meaning—and sometimes the search makes the treasure that much more enjoyable.

If I were asked to give a summary of how to study a book of the Bible, perhaps one of the Old Testament books with which I may not be as familiar, I would find an easier-to-read-version of the Bible, such as the New International Version, to get the message of the story. I have even used the Simple English Version, which I treat as a commentary on the passage because it is not really a translation. Reading it in this way gives me the storyline of the text. Then, I would go back and read more closely with the New American Standard in order to make sure the specific words and concepts were truly accurate. When teaching a class, I would always want to familiarize myself with other translations (such as King James Version, New Revised Version, etc.) in order that I might know how to handle comments or questions people in the class or congregation might ask.

The study of the Bible is the most rewarding study one will ever undertake. When we get together and study with others, it is amazing how much the insight of another person will impact your appreciation for and understanding of the Word of God.

Chapter 3 · *What You Should Know...*

- The Bible is a library of books rather than a single volume
- The chart depicting 'The Big Picture'
- the differences between the Old and New Testaments
- themes for each of the books of the Bible
- how one determines the best translation of the Bible to use.

4   THE STUDY OF CHRIST

Christology

There are many possible beginning points for discussing the life of Jesus. Since the Bible teaches that He was in existence before the creation of the world, the discussion could begin with exploring the concept of the Trinity. Then we know of the time when Jesus came to earth as a human, commonly referred to as the birth of Christ, or the incarnation. Another option would be to focus on the ministry of Jesus, which occurs from the time he was about 30 years of age. Another option would be to focus on the resurrection, ascension and enthronement of Jesus since the Biblical records of his crucifixion.

Each of these areas would not only be accurate, they would also be beneficial in describing the life of Christ.

The Authors of the Gospels

Let's start by first stepping back and looking at the biblical record that details Jesus' life from all four of these perspectives. The first four books of the New Testament (commonly referred to as the 'Gospels,' because they contain the 'good news' of Jesus Christ) represent our main source of information regarding the life of Jesus. Each book is written by different authors and represents a unique perspective on the Christ. The fact that we have four accounts helps to emphasize the importance of the story as well as helping to authenticate the story of Christ. Each author presents at least one side of the multifaceted nature of Jesus.

The authors themselves become part of the story. For example, Matthew is one of the original 12 apostles and is a tax-collector for the Roman authorities. The Romans were accustomed to conquering a land and immediately putting a member of the conquered people, in this case the Jews, in a position of collecting Roman taxes from their fellow countrymen. The Romans assumed that these people would be very familiar with who did have money and how much money had been earned in the barter of goods and other various transactions. Tax collectors were notoriously wealthy, most often because they collected more tax than was owed and pocketed the difference. Whether Matthew fits this description at the time Jesus called him will remain a mystery because the Scriptures provide no additional information.

Matthew would have been writing to Jews, however, shown by his appeal to those familiar with Hebrew history. He traces the lineage of Jesus back to Abraham, showing his Jewish heritage. He documents proof that Jesus is the Messiah, who fulfills prophecies of the Old Testament.

Mark, also known as John Mark, is not an apostle though he is well acquainted with them. He is initially a companion of Paul and Barnabas on the first missionary journey, but turns back very early in the journey. This disappoints Paul and eventually becomes a point of disagreement when Paul and Barnabas later determine to visit these same places on the next missionary journey. Barnabas accompanies John Mark on a separate journey from Paul, who chooses to travel with Silas. John Mark, for his part, not only earns the respect of Paul later because of the diligence of his work (2 Tim. 4:11), but is also close to the apostle Peter. Peter considers John Mark to be his "son," a term that doubtless refers to his faith relationship (1 Pet. 5:13).

Mark emphasizes the miracles of Jesus and shows him to be a man who quite literally serves the people. A key verse is Mark 10:45, where Mark quotes Jesus as describing his purpose as being a servant, epitomized by his willingness to go to the cross for the sins of the world.

Luke is called a physician by the apostle Paul (Col. 4:14) and is a person who travels extensively with Paul, perhaps caring for him, on his journeys. As the author of the gospel of Luke and the book of Acts (originally one volume but later separated) Luke frequently indicates his presence on parts of the journeys by inserting "we" in the text when present and referring to the group in third person ("they") when he was absent.

Luke writes to Theophilus with the expressed purpose of giving an orderly account of the events concerning Jesus Christ. With meticulous care and a polished style, he enumerates details of the life of Christ (Gospel of Luke) and the beginning of the church for which Jesus gave His life. His style seems directed to the intellectual and learned Greek audience to show that Jesus was the ideal and universal solution to man's greatest needs.

The author of the Gospel of John is one of the original twelve apostles, known as the apostle of love because of the way he describes himself in the gospel. Instead of self-references as "John" or "I," John chooses to use the phrase, "the disciple whom Jesus loved." As an eyewitness of the events he enumerates, his purpose statement can be found in John 20:30, 31, where he intends to convince readers that Jesus was indeed the Messiah, the son of the living God.

So, the four gospels seem to have four audiences in mind. Matthew seems to be writing for a Jewish audience. Mark seems to be addressing a non-Jewish audience, perhaps more specifically, the Romans. Luke seems to be addressing an intellectual, non-Jewish audience, perhaps the Greeks. And, John emphasizes the deity of Christ as he presents him as "the Son of God."

Omissions in the Accounts

These four accounts of the life of Jesus make no attempt to cover every event in Jesus' life. We have extremely limited information on his childhood with only details of his birth and events surrounding his trip to Jerusalem at the age of 12. Most of the information in the New Testament refers to the time that Jesus began his ministry, which Luke says was at about the age of 30. In writing his gospel, John even makes the statement that "there are also many other things which Jesus did, which if they were written in detail, I suppose that even the world itself would not contain the books which were written" (Jn. 21:25). The limited knowledge we have of Jesus does not mean that Jesus did not have a normal childhood, but rather the writers were emphasizing the relevant activities in His life that have an effect on our beliefs and practice.

The chronology of the events also did not seem to be important to the writers. Lack of clarity on specific events leaves scholars free to speculate on the exact time of the event. For example, in the cleansing of the temple, it is difficult to determine if the event took place at the beginning of his ministry (as Mark and John imply), or at the end of his earthly ministry (as Luke implies). Could this same scenario have occurred twice? These difficulties may never be solved to the satisfaction of every reader. And, the difference does not lessen the effect (or truth) of the text.

In addition, there is no physical description given of Jesus. What makes this most peculiar is that we have physical descriptions of men who lived long before Christ, such as Socrates, Aristotle, and Alexander the Great. But none of Jesus. Again, speculation causes us to wonder if there was a reason that physical descriptions are sparse. Could it have been that God wanted the images of Jesus to be limited to character descriptions and spiritual qualities as opposed to physical characteristics? Certainly we would agree that the spiritual qualities are paramount in our pursuit of Godliness. But the fact remains that very little is said about his physical traits.

Variations in the Four Accounts

When reading each gospel, we see differences in which particular areas the writers emphasize. Luke is the only author of the gospels who mentions that Jesus prayed all night before selecting the Twelve apostles. John is the only writer who describes Jesus' washing the disciples' feet.

In addition, there are several events that seem contradictory. Perhaps the authors were describing similar events, but not the same event, such as two records of the Sermon on the Mount. Perhaps there are contradictions and we are not able to fully understand them because of our lack of understanding of either the original text or actual events taking place in the specific time-period.

The World Into Which Christ Came

There is so much that occurs during the time of the events recorded in the Bible. It is very tempting to view the characters we read about in the Bible in somewhat of a mythical way, that is, never believing that secular events that we might have read about in history occurred simultaneously with the events recorded in the Bible. In addition, the Bible does not claim to be a book of sequential, chronological history nor do the Gospels claim to be biographies. They are documents carefully passed down from one generation to the next in order to share the story of God's people. They are primarily best termed 'documents of faith,' or documents upon which early believers and subsequent generations based their beliefs and their hopes.

It would be interesting to speculate as to why Jesus came at the time He did. It might seem to us that it would have been better for Him to come at a time when technology would have helped us more clearly record and preserve specific acts of teaching. Have you ever wondered why it was not possible for us to preserve in some way a means by which we could ascertain what Jesus looked like? Wouldn't it have been wonderful to have audio and/or visual recordings of the Sermon on the Mount or private conversations with believers? In this regard, we must trust the words that Paul spoke to the churches of Galatia when he said, "But when the right time came, God sent His Son" (Gal. 4:4).

What we do know about Jesus' coming is that a period of about 400 years passed between the prophecy of Malachi regarding the coming of the Messiah and the prophecies of John the Baptist, who would announce His coming. Perhaps this is why so many people were attracted to the desert to hear the prophecy of John—there had been such a lack of prophetic messages coming that people were hungering for divine direction. Some believe God wished to dramatize this important event or perhaps the delay was intentionally designed to make it more impressive. While this conclusion is speculative at best, we do know that God was certainly true to His word.

From a variety of sources (i.e., Apocryphal writings, writings of Josephus, a variety of Greek and Roman witnesses, archaeological findings and the Scriptures), we know many of the events that occurred during this 400 year interlude. This time period (425 B.C.–5 B.C.) would be an excellent subject for study—but it is not the focus of our study together.

To briefly summarize, the times into which the Christ appeared, we know that four empires preceded His coming. The Medo-Persian Period (539-333 B.C.) was followed by the Grecian Period (333-165 B.C.). For students of history, learning of Alexander the Great (333-323 B.C.), the Ptolemies (323-198 B.C.), the Seleucids (198-165 B.C.) provide excellent insight to the culture of the day. The Period of Independence (165-63 B.C.) is followed by the Roman Period (63 B.C.–A.D. 70), providing the desired

Divine timeframe for the Savior to be born.

Looking back from our perspective, we can see that several key events transpired that would have made this an ideal time. The Romans had achieved the *Pax Romana*, a time of relative peace in the land so that travel could be extended and communication over great distances was possible. They had also developed an extensive system of roads which allowed easier travel. The Greek language had become the language of commerce and so there was an excellent means of taking specific and accurate messages to a wide variety of people. Perhaps these might be some of the reasons that this time was chosen. The time for the coming of the Messiah had also been predicted to be in the days of the Roman kings by the prophet Daniel (Dan. 2:44). So, regardless of our reasoning and justification, it was providential that Christ would come when He did and in the manner in which He came.

Important Facts About Jesus As the Christ

Jesus in Prophecy

We do know about Jesus as the fulfillment of the promise for a Messiah when we read the Old and New Testaments. This is a crucial step and one that is taken for granted by those of us living in the 21st century. Had we been living in the 1st century, it would have been very difficult for many of us to accept that Jesus was the promised Messiah for several reasons. Primarily, the Jews were looking for a Messiah that would bring Israel back to national prominence. Their expectation was not for a quiet man of humble lineage to come in and work in such a way as not to call attention to himself. They expected a mighty leader, perhaps with soldiers, quite possibly with priestly credentials to redeem Israel. For Jesus to come from such obscurity and make such audacious claims certainly aroused suspicion and doubt among the religious leaders. For this redeemer to allow himself to be crucified was the final form of proof needed to show that he was an imposter.

To say that any honest Jew would have readily accepted Jesus as the Messiah is a vicious and indefensible charge. Saul of Tarsus was a leading Jew, a Pharisee nonetheless, and he was not convinced that Jesus was the Christ until he experienced the miraculous vision on the road to Damascus.

Once convinced, he became a tireless and selfless worker for the cause of Christ. Others believed once they weighed the evidence, including the study of the Law and the witnessing of the miracles.

From the perspective of the 21st century, however, we are able to compare Scriptures and see that Jesus did indeed meet the qualifications so established by prophets of old and confirmed by New Testament witnesses. Read the following Scriptures and you can see the evidence that seems so obvious to a Bible-believer now. Remember as you read, however, that those living in the 1st century did not have all the evidence that we now have in our possession.

Remember two things as we progress: (1) we must see for ourselves what the Bible says in order to learn these important truths, and (2) there is no substitute for opening up our Bibles and reading. You will be amazed at how your knowledge of God will grow and your faith in Him will increase as you spend time with the Scriptures.

Remember, we are focusing on Christ. The Bible predicts that a Messiah (a savior) will come. Jesus uniquely fits every prophecy in the Old Testament regarding the coming Messiah.

One of the most convicting proofs of the truths of the Bible is its predictive nature. We read in the Old Testament of something that will take place in the future and then we read of it occurring in the New Testament. The predictive nature of the Bible is a part of the proof of its truth.

The Old Testament Tells of Jesus

Jesus was alive at the beginning of the creation (Gen. 1:26; Heb. 1:1, 2).

Jesus described himself as the "I am," a term used by God to describe himself to Moses, and a statement used by Jesus which astounded and confounded the Jews listening to him (Ex. 3:14; John 8:58).

The reason for the first prophecy was to reveal that there was 'good news' for those that needed deliverance from the consequences of sin (Gen. 3:15).

Moses prophesied that the Jews should one day listen to a prophet that would come from their own countrymen (Deut. 18:15-19).

Matthew connects a prophecy of the coming Messiah (Isa. 7:14) with the birth of Jesus (Mt. 1:22-25).

The Old Testament closes with the prophecy of John the Baptist, who will usher in the Messiah (Mal. 4:5, 6).

The prophecy of the coming of John the Baptist and Jesus is said to have been fulfilled in the New Testament (Jn. 1:19-27; Mt. 11:14).

The story of the 'suffering servant' is a script for the life of Jesus (Isa. 53).

A specific time for the appearance of the kingdom is given by Daniel—in the days of the Roman kings (Dan. 2:31-45).

The Child Jesus

We read in the Gospels of the childhood of Jesus. We don't read many details, not nearly as many as we desire, but the picture that we read is sufficient to give us an indication of a life that was fairly typical of a Jewish boy up until the time that he began his ministry.

Jesus' birth was special because he was born to a young virgin named Mary. He was conceived by the Holy Spirit (Lk. 1:26-31).

Jesus was born in Bethelehem (Lk. 2:4-7).

King Herod learned that a king was born in Bethlehem, and he became highly suspicious (Mt. 2:1-3).

Jesus had at least four brothers and at least two sisters (Mk. 6:3).

He received a well-rounded childhood, evidenced by growth in four areas. He grew intellectually, physically, spiritually and socially (Lk. 2:41-52).

Jesus grew up in the home of a carpenter, Joseph (Mt. 13:55).

Jesus at 12 years old astounded the teachers in the temple with His knowledge and understanding (Jn. 2:46-48).

Jesus began his ministry when he was about 30 years of age (Lk. 3:23).

Jesus is Tempted

When we learn of Jesus, we learn of a person was fully human and fully divine. This is wonderful news because we learn that Jesus knows all about the temptations that we will face. Many texts of Scripture are useful for teaching us about these temptations.

Temptation is defined as being drawn away because of our own individual desires (James 1:12).

Jesus was led into the wilderness for the express purpose of being tempted by Satan (Mt. 4:1).

We know that God is not tempted with sin and does not tempt man with sin (James 1:13). This is also helpful in understanding how Jesus could be God and man. He was not tempted as God but rather as a man.

One of the occurrences that added to the temptation of Jesus was that he had been fasting for 40 days and nights and was hungry (Mt. 4:2).

The apostle John describes the three sources of appeal in temptation when he states that we are drawn to the world by the (1) lust of the eyes (2) lust of the flesh and (3) the pride of life (1 Jn. 2:15-17).

Jesus helps us understand how to handle temptation by showing us how he handled his temptations from Satan. He relied on the Scriptures and referred to it in time of temptation (Mt. 4:4, 7, 10).

When Jesus refused to give in to Satan, the devil left him for a time (Mt. 4:11).

We are comforted in temptation because we see that Jesus did not lash out in anger or revenge, but rather entrusted himself to God the Father and relied upon him for strength (1 Pet. 2:21-23).

Jesus had an advantage over Satan because he was knowledgeable of his ways and schemes (2 Cor. 2:11).

One blessing we have that should help us during temptation is the fact that God has full control over our temptation and will not allow us to be tempted above our level of strength. He promises to always provide a way of escape (1 Cor. 10:13).

Jesus Chooses His Apostles

Now Jesus has officially started his ministry. He is purposefully walking among the people, and it isn't long until we see what he has in mind.

Jesus prayed all night before he called his disciples to him and chose twelve of them to be his apostles (Lk. 6:12-13).

The apostles' personalities were starkly distinct. A character study of the twelve shows they are extreme opposites in personality. Their devotion to the Lord is noteworthy (Lk. 6:14-16).

There was one man, Paul, who was called as an apostle at a later time. He was not one of the original twelve but had a unique ministry, evidenced by the work of God in his life (1 Cor. 1:1; 15:8). Paul came to be an apostle by a special call from Jesus Christ (Gal. 1:1). His specific mission was to take the Gospel to the Gentiles (Rom. 15:15-16).

We could spend so much time just discussing the selection and training of the apostles themselves. Jesus spent a significant amount of time with these 12 men when they had only a partial conception of what Jesus had in mind. They simply knew that they believed he was the Messiah and they were intent on following him, even to the point of death. Indications are that they anticipated an earthly kingdom, but as the time for his sacrificial death on the cross approached, Jesus would begin to be more specific in his private conversations about what was to take place.

I am encouraged by the fact that, though these men did not know everything the coming of Jesus entailed, they were faithful to the cause and open to his corrective teaching. One, we know, would betray Jesus. Jesus seems to have been aware of the impending betrayal from the beginning.

The Painful Experiences in Jerusalem

Finally the time comes when Jesus' ministry has been completed, and he moves toward Jerusalem for the last time. The time was so brief, perhaps 2 ½ to 3 years. But in that time, he had accomplished everything necessary for his kingdom to come to fruition and for the apostles to lead the faithful to a glorious ministry.

Notice the innocence of Jesus and the pressure under which Pilate made his decision to convict him. As you read the accounts, you'll be reminded of the audacious statements made about the Son of God and the willpower necessary for Jesus not to obliterate all those who were falsely accusing him. Since God cannot co-exist with sin, how much endurance must it have required of him not to do away with his false accusers?

Each of the Gospels describes the series of events from the trial through the resurrection in unique ways. The same events are described in subtly distinctive ways.

Matthew views Jesus as the Messiah because he was writing to a Jewish audience. He vividly describes the betrayal, arrest and trial of Jesus with great attention to the disrespect that Jesus received from the Jews.

Mark describes the events leading up to the crucifixion with great attention to the progression of events. He numbers the days and more clearly shows the last week of Jesus' life than do the other writers. His description has a dark tone and focuses on the dramatic presentation of who Jesus was.

Luke, the physician, surprisingly gives less description of the physical experience of enduring a crucifixion. His brief description of the crucifixion is summed up in one phrase, "And when they came to the place called The Skull, there they crucified him and the criminals, one on the right and the other on the left." Perhaps we would be expecting more regarding the physical side, but Luke is insistent on giving an orderly account of events that transpired.

John picks up on stories and perspectives the other Gospel writers have left out. Since his purpose is to convince his readers that Jesus is the Christ (Jn. 20:30-31), he tells stories that emphasize the response of people to the fact of the crucifixion.

Each of the accounts shows a different perspective on the suffering of Jesus. We come away from these stories with a renewed sense of profound amazement at the extent to which Jesus went to give the appropriate sacrifice to save mankind.

The Resurrection of Jesus

We should be careful not to overlook the response of initial shock and disbelief on the part of those realizing Jesus had been raised. Little wonder as to why people would have been shocked. Perhaps those who believed that Jesus was the Messiah never did expect him to be killed in the first place. After all, here was a man who could heal the sick, cast out demons, raise the dead, miraculously produce food to feed thousands, and control the wind and the rain. How could he allow someone to take his life?

Once his life was taken, you can imagine the disbelief at hearing that he was dead, only to be followed by extreme joy and exaltation in the fact that he had been raised from the dead. What a roller-coaster of emotions!

The Second Coming

The next event on the horizon for the world is the second coming of Christ. We know from the Scriptures that Jesus came the first time to this world to give his life as a ransom for the sins of mankind. He will come the second time to receive the faithful into his presence forever.

We should not forget that Jesus said he was going to prepare a place and would come back for his children to be with them forever (Jn. 14:2-3).

We will know when Jesus comes because every eye will see him when he comes in the sky (Rev. 1:7).

One thing we know for sure is that we do not know for sure when he is coming (Mt. 24:42-43).

Those Christians who are alive at his coming will have their bodies transformed instantaneously from a physical body (mortal) to a spiritual body (immortal) (1 Cor. 15:51-53).

When the Lord comes in the sky, those Christians who have died will come with the Lord in the air (1 Thess. 4:16).

When the Lord comes again, this earth and all the elements of the earth will burn away with a fervent heat (2 Pet. 3:10-11).

Our Responsibility

The Bible is fairly specific when it speaks of the second coming. There are specific issues mentioned in great detail. However, the emphasis in the Bible does not seem to be on the eternal reward or punishment as it does on the responsibility of God's people to live faithfully while still on the earth.

The Bible teaches us that there is only one resurrection. Those who are faithful will have the resurrection of life. Those who have not believed and committed evil deeds will have the resurrection of judgment (Jn. 5:28-29).

The Bible also graphically depicts the judgment scene when all of mankind will stand before the judgment seat in order to receive the pronouncement of reward or punishment (Mt. 25:31-36). The Bible's explicit description of Hell makes it a place that is repugnant to the serious thinker (Rev. 21:8).

The importance of knowing the life of Christ is not just an academic exercise. It impacts each of our lives on a physical and spiritual level. We live for the Lord on earth because our desire is to live with the Lord for eternity.

Chapter 4 · *What You Should Know...*

· the authors for each of the gospels

· why the gospel accounts are different

· the birth and childhood events in Jesus' life

· the circumstances surrounding Satan tempting Jesus

· the process of selecting the apostles

· the events surrounding the crucifixion of Jesus.

5   THE STUDY OF MAN

Anthropology

You would be thoroughly amazed if I were able to summarize the origin, existence and future of man in one short chapter, wouldn't you? Of course, that would be impossible. Historians, archaeologists, scholars and intellectuals have spent entire lifetimes dedicated to determining the history of one aspect of mankind—and their findings have frequently been added to the collection of inconclusive research. It isn't that their work was futile or unnecessary, because their work was very helpful in uncovering one more layer of inspection that is helpful to mankind.

It is possible, however, to look back at what we have discovered regarding the history of man and be able to dispel some false assumptions that are promoted as facts. The challenge is to sift through artifacts and try to analyze the origin, meaning and purpose of various 'pieces of the puzzle,' and draw conclusions on what might be our history. This process, particularly the work of archeologists, requires a great deal of knowledge, imagination and humility in that our conclusions may at best be 'educated guesses.'

Strangely, some historians argue with themselves. In one series, *A History of the Western World*, the editor (Shepard B. Clough) says, "Our knowledge of the prehistoric world must be based entirely on archaeological evidence; it grows progressively dimmer as we move back from the threshold of history and as evidence becomes scarcer" (*The*

Appearance of Civilization, D.C. Heath & Company, Boston, 1964, p. 15).

In the next volume of the series, the same editor says, "The earliest appearance of civilization has not yet been determined by scholars, and it is only in recent years that the historian and particularly the archaeologist has gradually worked his way back of the limit imposed by the existence of written documents into the prehistoric world. But with each generation our knowledge of the era preceding the invention of writing has become more precise" (*The Beginning of Civilization*, D.C. Heath & Co., 1965, p. 11). Though this example is dated, it illustrates the dilemma of historians determining with great accuracy the specific acts of ancient peoples.

To add to the legion of historians, archaeologists and scholars, all detectives of trying to determine man's beginning, we add Will Durant whose eleven volume series on civilization certainly sounds an optimistic note. He says, "There is no telling what vistas of civilization and history will be opened up when the ground has been worked, and the material studied..." (The Story of Civilization, vol. 1, p. 119). So we see an ongoing attempt to determine man's origin amidst speculation, archaeology and critique. Should we find it any less strange that man is still questioning and critiquing the origins of belief in God?

With that understanding, we now turn to consider the origin of man and focus our emphasis on the origin of religion. Hans-Joachim Schoeps, a German Jewish scholar and author of *The Religions of Mankind*, identified an intriguing concept of the origin of religion. Len Woods says,

Not so long ago, people didn't so much "choose" their religion, as it chose them. Religion was, in large part, a function of one's geography. To be Irish meant to be Catholic. If you were Saudi-born, you practiced Islam. If you grew up in rural north Alabama, odds were you would become a Pentecostal long before you would even know about, much less worship in, an Episcopalian church.

Now, due largely to television, the internet, and increased proselytizing, religion has gone global. A Hindu teenager living in Bangalore decides to become a Mormon. A businesswoman in suburban Chicago converts to Buddhism. Like a spiritual shopping mall, numerous religious belief systems are "open for business." A few are massive, ancient, and unchanging; many others are small, recent, and very fluid in their theology. Indeed, the religious landscape is cluttered, complex, and ever-changing.

Religions of Mankind (p. vi)

We now have a myriad of choices regarding religion. There seems to be more and more distinct religious groups appearing on the scene. Reflective of this is the fact that Frank S. Mead and Samuel S. Hill are now in their eleventh edition of *Handbook of Denominations in the United States*. There also seems to be more vocal (print and campus-wide discussions) opposition to organized religion, illustrated by the pronounced efforts of agnostics, such as popular authors Christopher Hitchens, Richard Dawkins and others.

Basically, if we do have choices about religion, where do we go for an authoritative response? How can we even discuss the subject without the conversation turning into a debate or argument?

Three Key Questions

I would suggest that there are three key questions upon which we must agree—or we had better not even try to have a discussion. In other words, if we cannot agree on these three answers, our conversation will result in nothing more than swapping of opinions and theories, but no reason to change our minds.

The first question is, "Do you believe in God?" If we cannot agree there is a Creator of the universe whom we will define as God, we will have very little chance for a productive discussion. If I don't believe in God, I also beg the question of, "What do you believe in?" If I do not believe in a Creator of this universe, I must answer the query of how did what we know is in existence, get here?

The second question is, "Do you believe in Jesus as God's son?" Many people believe in God but do not believe that Jesus is the son of God. In fact, many spiritual and God-fearing people do not believe in Jesus as God's son. But to deny Jesus as the son of God is to say that (1) Jesus fabricated the stories about his pre-existence and his divine mission, (2) that Jesus was just a normal mortal like the rest of us and the story of his resurrection from the dead is not true, (3) that we are still living with the guilt of sin because the atoning blood of his sacrificial death did not take away the sins of the world, and (4) we agree with the apostle Paul that "if there is no resurrection of the dead, we are of all men most to be pitied" (1 Cor. 15:19).

This does not mean that we reason backwards and affirm that Jesus is the Son of God because of our need. That wouldn't make it so. We rather must first give more careful consideration to the teachings of the Bible to see if Jesus indeed was the son of God and then consider the implications of that fact on our lives.

The third question is just as vital as the first two. "Do you believe that the Bible is the authoritative will of God?" If a person says that he believes in God—and even believes in Jesus as God's son, but will not let the Bible be the source of authority for our lives, he will have difficulty explaining just exactly what is authoritative. That will be the issue that will continue to resurface. What will we use for our source for authority in our faith and practice? Now if we can agree on the answers to those three questions, our time will not be wasted and we have the potential of learning together what God desires and how we can fulfill his desires in our lives.

Sources of Authority in the Bible

When I speak of authority, I am referring to having the ability to depend on the message given as having a source that is completely trustworthy. It is listening to a message that you can rest assured will be true—for now and evermore. This is very important because we all receive (and frequently give) information that we later find to be untrustworthy. It wasn't because the source of the comment was necessarily intentionally misleading; it was just that they received false information and believed it to be true. Now there are some people that are intentionally misleading for a variety of reasons—but we don't have the time to deal with all of those issues.

Of interest to us in our study of the Bible is the securing of something that is completely trustworthy. It seems that in giving us the Bible, God implied that there were some things that

What is authoritative?

- Words of the Old Testament.
- Teachings of Jesus.
- Words of the Holy Spirit.
- Words of the Apostles.

were completely trustworthy. In fact, he even implies that the inspired Word ('God-breathed' words or 'sacred writings' that we call Scripture) has been closed. That is, we are not waiting for more words from God on how a Christian should live. If it was the case that more instruction from God was needed to live the Christian life, then Paul's words to Timothy (2 Tim. 3:16-17) that the man of God is "complete, thoroughly furnished unto every good work" (or entirely prepared for every good work) would be false.

In case you're wondering if there might be another book that we have overlooked over all the centuries that God intended to be added to the Bible, you can rest assured that we have all that we need. Neale Pryor, Bible professor at Harding University, was asked once what he thought of the chances of finding another text. His reply was that if one were found, it would have to be consistent with the revealed Word that is already given or we would know it to be false. If it agreed with everything that we have in the Bible, then it wouldn't be necessary. Either way, we know we have the truth.

There are four indications in the Bible itself that its words are authoritative. The first part of the Bible we know to be true is the Old Testament. In 1 Corinthians 10:1, Paul identifies the stories of the Israelites as they were wandering in the wilderness. Paul details their problems and the sources of their problems, including a gradual, progressive movement away from God. He identifies how they moved from evil cravings (v. 6), to idolatry (v. 7), to immoral acts (v. 8), to trying the Lord (v. 9), to grumbling (v. 10) which led to their destruction (v. 10). Twice in this text Paul says these things happened as an example for us. This is fairly positive proof of the authoritative nature of the Old Testament Scriptures. In addition, Paul repeats this caution in Romans 15:4 when he tells the church at Rome to pay attention to "whatever was written in earlier times" as being very instructive in developing perseverance, finding encouragement and gaining hope.

A Progressive Fall Described:

- Evil cravings (1 Cor. 10:6)
- Idolatry (1 Cor. 10:7)
- Immoral acts (1 Cor. 10:7)
- Trying God (1 Cor. 10:9)
- Grumbling (1 Cor. 10:10)
- Destruction (1 Cor. 10:10)

We don't just "fall into sin."

The second area that is authoritative is represented by the teachings of Jesus. In 1 Corinthians 7:10, Paul is addressing a pressing issue in the Corinthian church regarding marriage. In the midst of his instruction, he pauses to add credence to his message. He says, "But to the married I give instruction, not I, but the Lord…" This was not to diminish any words that he said as not being authoritative, because on other occasions he would cite his authoritative position as an apostle In 1 Corinthians 1:1, he says that he was "called as an apostle" and in 2 Corinthians 11:5, he says that he is "not in the least inferior to the most eminent apostles." But there was special significance in the teaching because it came from the Lord.

Paul also quotes the words of Jesus himself in 1 Timothy 5:18, when Luke quotes the words of Jesus (Luke 10:7), and Paul calls them "Scripture." This not only tells us that Jesus words are "sacred" (Scripture meaning 'sacred writings') but also that the words of Luke are considered to be inspired.

In 1 Thessalonians 4:15, Paul comforts a young church in the city of Thessalonica who seems to be concerned about faithful saints who have died and are possibly missing the reward from God. Paul comforts them with words that he said he received from the Lord himself. From Paul, these words not only were authoritative for himself but also instructive for all Christians.

Of course, Jesus Himself claimed that His words were authoritative. In the Sermon on the Mount (Mt. 5-7), He referred to the Old Testament and then added His unique, authoritative perspective. It was immediately recognizable to His listeners, for Matthew says that at the end of the sermon, they were all amazed because He spoke "as one having authority"—which, of course, is quite an understatement. He *is* the authority.

A third source that is authoritative is the Holy Spirit. In John 16:13-14, Jesus was telling of the coming of the Holy Spirit as He described His work as that of a guide. Of course, Jesus was speaking to the apostles (the Twelve) about how the Spirit would work in their lives.

In another Scripture, the apostle Peter is testifying that the words of the prophets were not of their own invention when he says, "no prophecy was ever made by an act of human will, but men moved by the Holy Spirit spoke from God" (2 Pet. 1:21). Peter knew that men could not accurately interpret God's will without divine help.

While Jesus was alive on the earth, training his apostles, preparing them for his upcoming departure, he told of the work of the Holy Spirit. He was speaking to his apostles alone in John 14-16 (an important point to make to those that believe everything said in these chapters applies to all Christians for all time). He described the work of the Holy Spirit to be to guide them (primary application to the apostles) into all the truth. In that same setting, he had previously said (Jn. 14:26) that the Holy Spirit would 'bring to their remembrance' all that had been said to them. How reassuring it must have been to know that the words they were speaking were given to them by God Himself, in the form of the Holy Spirit.

Finally, we know that the words of the apostles themselves are authoritative. Paul recognized this on at least two occasions. In Ephesians 3, he outlined his understanding of the 'mystery' of his ministry. He gives what has been termed a 'chain of revelation' which begins with (1) a mystery, (2) a revealing of the mystery to Paul, (3) Paul writing down his understanding of the mystery, and (4) our reading of his writings which leads to our understanding the will of God. Paul was so sure of this message that he understood that it was his calling to take the message of the mystery (which here is that God was now reaching out beyond the Jews to the Gentiles with the saving message of grace) to the entire world. It was to be made known through the church. We can readily see the excitement of Paul and should reflect that same sense of energy and urgency.

> ### Chain of Revelation (Eph. 3):
> · There is a mystery.
> · Mystery revealed to Paul.
> · Paul writes revelation down.
> · We read the written word.
> · We understand the mystery.

Paul was grateful when others recognized this genuine power. He wrote to the church at Thessalonica and expressed his gratitude that they not only accepted his teaching, but that they accepted it for what it was—the word of God (1 Thess. 2:13).

General Revelation vs. Divine Revelation

There are some things that are so obvious that we concede their existence. For example, I know that the earth exists—along with the sun, moon and stars. I've seen them. I've experienced them. But how they came to be here is another story.

General revelation is that knowledge we have because it is so obvious to everyone. What is not so obvious is its origin. The Psalmist said, "The heavens declare the glory of God and the firmament shows his handiwork" (Psa. 19:1). The Psalmist implied that anyone would have to know that there is a God because God has revealed himself by the entire creation. Macrospace viewed through a telescope and microspace viewed through a microscope all attest to the fact that God has created a wonderful world.

Paul wrote to the church at Rome that "since the creation of the world His (God's) invisible attributes, His eternal power and divine nature, have been clearly seen, being understood through what has been made, so that they are without excuse" (Rom. 1:20). Paul builds a case that people in the first century knew about God—they had to know about some Creator simply by looking around at the created world. The evidence was overwhelming enough so as to make them responsible for their actions.

There is, however, another kind of revelation—one that is not as obvious but just as convincing. It is divine revelation, where God intentionally and effectively reveals his will to humans so that his creation might know more about God and their relationship to him. This revelation is given assuredly at the discretion of God himself—no sooner or later. From reading the Bible, it is evident that God chose to reveal certain aspects of his nature according to a certain plan. For example, Jesus did not come until the time was exactly right (Gal. 4:4).

Do you need more examples? In John, chapters 14-16, Jesus tells the apostles he is about to leave them. They, of course, did not understand. He explains to them that he must leave in order that the 'comforter' (the Holy Spirit) would come to do his work (we'll discuss the work of the Holy Spirit in a subsequent chapter). But the important point here is that Jesus was revealing some information to them—then telling them that more information would be divinely given to them at a later point. This, of course, happened as we read in other New Testament passages.

In addition, Paul explains the process of receiving divine revelation in Ephesians 3:1-6 (as discussed earlier) and 1 Corinthians 2:6-16. Peter mentions "a faith of the same kind as ours" when he writes to Christians facing turbulent times (2 Pet. 1:1). Jude writes a succinct letter to individuals warning them to "contend earnestly for the faith which was once for all delivered to the saints" (Jude 3). This is an indication that Peter and Jude recognized a specific body of knowledge or information that was deemed to be "the faith" applicable to all Christians.

Summary

To bring it all together we must realize that man was created by God, according to the Bible, with the responsibility to recognize his Creator as the sovereign God of the universe. This God has revealed himself through both general and divine revelation and man has the responsibility and privilege to honor his deity.

From a secular perspective, the Bible is one belief among many. This great variety of beliefs can be easily viewed as myths invented by various peoples seeking to find something beyond themselves for meaning. Antagonistic agnostics will look with scorn at those who believe that one singular God created the world. The myths are portrayed as fabrications of a wild imagination and regularly and openly ridiculed.

But the agnostic and atheist still struggle with proving scientifically the issues already discussed in this book—primarily the beginning of life itself. Offering nothing more than conjecture and hypotheses that continually change with each passing discovery, many skeptics cannot disprove the fact that the story of the Bible has survived countless generations of mankind and numberless attacks upon its credibility and substantiation.

The history of man begins with the search for answers and will continue until the end of time. The Bible tells us that one day it will all be revealed. Until that time, the following Old Testament passage may serve as the best summary of our lives.

"The secret things belong to the Lord our God, but the things revealed belong to us and to our sons forever..."   *Deuteronomy 29:29*

Chapter 5 · *What You Should Know...*

- · the 3 key questions necessary for productive discussion.
- · the 4 sources of authority found in the Bible.
- · Paul's description of a 'chain of revelation.'
- · the difference between general revelation and divine revelation.
- · the difference between faith and 'the faith.'

6   THE STUDY OF SIN

Hamartiology

One of the most noticeable words used in conjunction with religion, and arguably one of the more contested, is the word sin. As discussed in Chapter 1, the word sin comes from the Greek word *hamartia*, which simply means 'missing the mark.' The best mental image for me is to imagine an archer shooting an arrow toward a target and missing the bull's-eye. The target has been set by God, and the one who attempts to hit the target misses frequently. From this we get the idea of sinning, or continually missing the target. The reason that sin is such a hotly debated topic is the simple belief that because man doesn't agree on the target.

The first occurrence of a sin—as we're describing it—is found in the book of Genesis. There are a variety of views on the residual effects of Adam's sin. In other words, what is the specific penalty that mankind incurs because of the sin in the Garden of Eden? The study of the consequences of Adam's sin and the consequences of our sin represents an enormous amount of time and effort on the part of scholars trying to decide how sin impacts us. While we will not have sufficient time in this book to detail all the issues, let me at least give an idea of the scope of the conversation. The questions might include:

1. Do we inherit the guilt of Adam's sin when we are born?
2. Can man do anything that will allow God to forgive these sins?
3. Has God already deemed some guilty of sin, whatever they do?

5. Has God already chosen some who will be saved regardless of what they do?
6. Does the Bible teach a "plan of salvation?"
7. Are we saved by the 'plan' or the 'man?'
8. If every man was born a sinner, does this make Jesus a sinner from his birth?

I would like to address each of these questions—and will to some degree. But as you can see, we could spend so much time on each aspect of these questions that we would be negligent of the first task at hand—which is learning about sin.

Before we address these questions, I would like to explore a more specific example of sin as described in the Bible. Then, I would like to point out how numerous Biblical authors describe a progression of sin. We will look at the fact taught in the Bible that sin was the reason for the coming of Christ—and subsequently implies and details how Jesus is the only remedy for sin. How that works is the most astounding story in the Bible and the message that needs to resonate within each person.

What is Sin?

There are several ways of looking at sin because in the most basic sense, sin, as we have defined it, occurs when we 'miss the mark' that God has set for us. The Bible mentions several specific ways of understanding sin. First, the apostle John defines sin by saying that "everyone who practices sin also practices lawlessness; and sin is lawlessness" (1 Jn. 3:4). Sin, then, is breaking the law. I see what the law is, and I knowingly break it. One person said it is like drawing a line in the sand—and daring someone to step over it. I deliberately 'step over the line.'

In the same letter, John also gives another definition of sin. He says that "all unrighteousness is sin" (1 Jn. 5:17). If righteousness is defined as actions that would be in harmony with the will of God, then every act that is outside the will of God is sin.

A third way of looking at sin is found in Paul's letter to the church at Rome. He says, "whatever is not from faith is sin" (Rom. 14:23). In this particular letter Paul had been discussing a disagreement over opinions, or doubtful points, regarding eating meat. It seems many Christian Jews were having difficulty leaving the Law of Moses behind when they came to Christ. They believed that eating meat that had been offered to idols, as the pagans did, was a sin. Paul knew that there was nothing wrong with the meat itself, but he also knew the problems it was causing in the church. He concluded by saying that if you could not act in such a way that was consistent with your beliefs, it would be a sin. So, we would conclude today that for any person to act in a way they truly believe would be outside the will of God, it would be a sin for them to continue in that act.

A fourth and final way we will explore the perspectives of sin is a statement made by James, the half-brother of Jesus, when he writes a letter to Jews who believed in Christ. He encourages their spiritual growth and then concludes by saying that "to one who knows the right thing to do, and does not do it, to him it is sin" (Jas. 4:17). Now, after listening to James, I know that according to the Bible I am supposed to act on what I know to be right. If I fail in that regard, I am held accountable.

What does all this mean? Simply this. Regardless of how we live, each one of us will sin. We may step over the line and break a law of God. We may commit acts that are not in accordance with his will and sin. We may do certain things, knowing when we do them that they are wrong. We may even have doubts about what we are doing—and do them anyway. We may fail to do something that we know we should have done. Regardless of how we act—we are going to sin. We are going to 'miss the mark.' The conclusion is that we all need to face the fact that we sin.

One more thought before you close this book in despair. God *knew* that we would sin. That does *not* mean that he *makes* us sin. It means that he *knew* we would sin. The difference between *knowing* that we would sin (foreknowledge) and *making* us sin (predestined) is tremendously significant. But before we discuss the distinctions, let's look a little more at what the Bible says about sin.

The Process of Sin

The Bible shows that there is a process that we go through when we sin. It isn't as though we just wake up and begin sinning. We actually move through a series of small steps that spiral progressively worse until we find ourselves in a state of habitual sin. If we could just step back and remain objective, we could see how the process unfolds. But we are usually too close to the situation to recognize the problem—so we are not alarmed.

Sin occurs when desire, temptation and opportunity come together. One man has described the process as the attraction, the deception, the preoccupation, the conception, the subjection, and finally, the desperation of sin. That is a complex way of looking at a simple yet mind boggling concern. We know that something is not condoned by God—and yet we stay so close to it that it finally begins to linger on our minds until we give in. The Bible describes it in a variety of ways.

The basic premise is detailed by the apostle John when he says, "Do not love the world, nor the things in the world. If anyone loves the world, the love of the Father is not in him. For all that is in the world, the lust of the flesh and the lust of the eyes and the boastful pride of life, is not from the Father, but is from the world. And the world is passing away, and also its lusts; but the one who does the will of God abides forever" (1 Jn. 2:15-17). Here is a list of three ways we sin: (1) the lust of the flesh, (2) the lust of the eyes, and (3) the boastful pride of life. One man shortened it by saying that we face "the three G's." If you are a guy, you must face *girls, gold and glory*. For girls, it would be *guys, gold and glory*. Regardless, these are the three areas that have historically trapped mankind.

For example, Eve faced temptation in the Garden of Eden. The Bible says, "When the woman saw that the tree was good for food, and that it was a delight to the eyes, and that tree was desirable to make one wise, she took from its fruit and ate" (Gen. 3:6). She was so deceived by the serpent that she asked the wrong questions. She was asking, "Is it good to eat?" Could that be the lust of the flesh? She asked, "Is it lovely?" Could that be the lust of the eyes? She asked, "Will it do anything for me?" Could this be the pride of life? Many believe that she was dealing with the same issues that each of us must face when we are confronted with opportunities to sin. Will we obey God, or do we choose to stray?

Another example is given in the first Psalm. The Psalmist says "Blessed is the man that does not walk in the counsel of the ungodly, nor stand in the way of sinners, nor sit in the seat of the scornful" (Psa. 1:1). There is a progression of walking—to standing—to sitting. The blessed man does not begin the process.

A final example is given by the apostle Paul when he writes to the church at Corinth. He warns them to remember the Israelites as they were released from Egyptian bondage (1 Cor. 10:1-13). He notes their systematic, progressive movement away from God by noting their "craving evil things," to becoming "idolaters," to "acting immorally," to "trying the Lord," to "starting to speak their thoughts," or grumbling. Paul says it didn't happen overnight—and the church at Corinth was to remember this lesson as being instructive.

Practical Application

The book of Romans is fascinating for numerous reasons. But one of the most interesting aspects of the book is to step back and see what Paul is trying to say to a church He planned to visit. When we read the entire letter, we learn that he has never been there (Rom. 1:13), and yet he seems to know so many people that are in the church (Rom. 16). In his letter, he seems to give a summary perspective of how God works in the lives of Christians. It is a fascinating study—one that has consumed the lives of numerous scholars and authors. For our purposes, I would like for us to see what Paul says about sin.

Let's just walk through the book of Romans and take note of specific times when Paul mentions man's propensity to sin—and the subsequent response of God.

The first stop is in Romans 1, where Paul insists that *man knows better* than to sin. He says that the creation itself testifies to the fact that there is a God—so man is without excuse in recognizing God (Rom. 1:20). In the same text, he identifies the same "process" of moving away from God. Man knows about God (v. 20), he chooses to ignore God (vv. 21, 22), he begins to indulge in sin (vv. 24-27), and finally reaches a point of no return where he participates with delight in sinful activities (vv. 28-32).

Paul then asserts that *man needs redemption* when he says, "For all have sinned and fallen short of the glory of God" (Rom. 3:23). Paul acknowledges in this letter that both Jews and Gentiles have sinned—which means all of mankind has sinned and fallen short. That phrase 'fallen short' takes on new meaning when we understand the definition of sin to be 'missing the mark.'

Paul then explains that *God acts on man's behalf.* He begins by asking in Romans 4:3, "What does the Scripture say?" He spends the rest of this chapter answering this question. He describes what happens in verse 4—

righteousness is given. He explains how it happened in verse 9—through faith. He explains why it happened in verse 24—because of our needs. Now that Paul has described what God has done, *man has reason to rejoice*—and this is just what he explains in Romans 5. Paul says we rejoice in the hope of the glory of God (5:2) and we rejoice in our tribulations (5:3) because we see that this process is working to make us stronger in our faith. Finally, Paul says we rejoice in God (5:11) because we have received reconciliation (forgiveness for our sin) through Jesus Christ. Good reasons to rejoice!

In my opinion, Romans 6 is the most outstanding description of the transformative process of conversion in the entire Bible. *Man acts and God responds.* The penitent believer is baptized for the forgiveness of his sins, and God makes him a new person. The new life is given during the submissive act of baptism. The transformation of a sinner (person who stands convicted of sin) into a saint (a child of God) is compared to the sacrifice of Jesus in which he died, was buried, and rose from the dead. There is a death (man dies to his old habits by confessing that he was wrong and now wants to turn to a new life), he is baptized into Christ (a burial into the death of Christ), and rises from the watery grave as a new man (like the resurrection of Jesus from the dead). God then declares that he is a new man and has been washed of all his sins. It is a beautiful picture that is more than a symbol. It is an inspired account as to how God views conversion.

Romans 7 is a gripping story of Paul describing man's trying to live the Christian life. *Man struggles* with the fact that regardless of how much he struggles against sin—it seems he is not able to completely rid himself of it. The things that he wants to do are not done. The actions that he does not want to do are the very things that he does. What a tremendous battle! He finally looks up in despair and says, "Who will set me free from the body of this death?" The answer comes in the first verse of Romans 8. Paul tells us that *God pardons* us because of our connection with the sacrifice of Jesus Christ.

In Romans 10, Paul doesn't hesitate to tell us that *God reminds* us of our dependence on Him. He is writing to baptized believers when he says, "whoever shall call upon the name of the Lord shall be saved" (Rom. 10:13). He is not writing to non-believers. He is writing to Christians. He calls them "saints" in Romans 1:7 and describes their conversion in Romans 6:1-7.

Paul spends a significant portion of Scripture (Rom. 12) in describing how a Christian should live. *Man learns* that he has responsibility to God and to other people. And, as if it is needed, Paul ends his letter speaking about how *the church serves God* by serving others (Rom. 16). It is a wonderful story of redemption that applies to each one of us.

Is it possible to summarize the story of the Bible in one concise statement? Let me try.

> **God's relationship with man described in book of Romans**
>
> · Man knows better (ch. 1)
> · Man needs redemption (ch. 3)
> · God acts...man benefits (ch. 5)
> · Man rejoices (ch.6)
> · Man struggles (ch. 7)
> · God pardons (ch. 8)
> · God reminds (ch. 10)
> · Man learns (ch. 12)
> · The church serves (ch. 16).

The reason for the coming of Christ is 'sin.' The only remedy for sin is the blood of Jesus Christ. The purpose of proclaiming this word is so that the message can be "made known to all the nations, leading to obedience of faith; to the only wise God, through Jesus Christ, be the glory forever. Amen" (Rom. 15:25).

Now, did you catch the methodology that Paul reveals in his letter to the Romans? It is subtle but very significant. When it comes to sin, *man knows better* (chapter 1), *man needs redemption* (chapter 3), *God acts and man benefits* (chapter 4), *man rejoices* (chapter 5), *man acts and God responds* (chapter 6), *man struggles* (chapter 7), *God pardons* (chapter 8), *God reminds* (chapter 10), *man learns* (chapter 12), and *the church serves* (chapter 16).

We should not rush through this discussion without emphasizing the fact that God did not leave us without guidance. There are four benefits of the Scriptures that help us in our battle against sin.

Paul writes to Timothy and tells him that people in the world in which he was living were growing progressively worse (2 Tim. 3:1-9). That would have been discouraging news. Paul says, however, that Timothy had been entrusted with teaching that would help him endure difficulty and work efficiently for the cause of Christ. That teaching, described in the latter part of the chapter (2 Tim. 3:10-17) would provide everything that he would need to persevere and endure difficult days. He says:

All Scripture is given by inspiration of God and is profitable for doctrine, reproof, correction, for instruction in righteousness that the man of God may be perfect, thoroughly furnished unto every good work.   2 Tim. 3:16,17

Paul identifies these four benefits of scripture as being beneficial for (a) doctrine (teaching what is right), (b) reproof (teaching what is wrong, (c) correction (teaching how to get right), and (d) instruction in righteousness (teaching how to stay right). This would have been a wonderful assurance to Timothy in the first century and it is just as applicable now in the 21st century.

Answers to the 7 Questions

But I told you earlier that I would address seven questions that seem to bother us. I wish I had more time to spend digging into the background of these questions. Many of these will be addressed later, but here are some brief responses that we should address now.

1. Do we inherit the guilt of Adam's sin when we are born?

No, we do not inherit the guilt of Adam's sin. The Bible teaches that we inherit the consequences of his sin—which is physical death. Each time a person dies, we should be reminded of the sin of Adam. Romans 4 and 5 are helpful to our understanding this.

2. Can man do anything that will allow God to forgive these sins?

Man cannot save himself nor can he perform enough great acts to 'earn' a place in Heaven. However, God has provided a way for a man who chooses to serve God to be forgiven of his sins. Read John 1:12 and see that God gives us the "right" to become 'sons of God.'

3. Has God already deemed that some are guilty of sin regardless of what they do?

No, God has given us freedom to choose and he desires that all of us will choose to follow Him (2 Pet. 3:9). If someone has told you that it has already been determined who will go to Heaven or not, they need to honestly address Scriptures that emphasize man's choice in areas of belief and the attending consequences for poor choices made.

4. Has God already chosen some who will be saved regardless of what they do?

No, that would mean that God has already chosen some to be lost and we know that is not the case. If you have been convinced that you have no hope, let me say—the Bible has a different message.

5. Does the Bible teach a "plan of salvation?"

A plan of salvation, defined as a desired path for man to travel in order to make contact with the blood of Christ, is clearly taught in the Bible. This will be discussed in later chapters.

6. Are we saved by the 'plan' or the 'man?'

Yes. By both the man (Jesus Christ) and the plan (living according to His will).

7. If every man was born a sinner, does this make Jesus a sinner from his birth?

If every man was born a sinner, then Jesus would have to be a sinner because he was a man (Heb. 4:15). We know that he was both God and man. We'll discuss this in later chapters.

Perhaps this is helpful in identifying sin. In the next chapter, we will look at how the Bible says we can be 'saved' from the penalty of the sins each of us commit.

part of the story. For example, Matthew is one of the original 12 apostles and is a tax-collector for the Roman authorities. The Romans were accustomed to conquering a land and immediately putting a member of the conquered people, in this case the Jews, in a position of collecting Roman taxes from their fellow countrymen. The Romans assumed that these people would be very familiar with who did have money and how much money had been earned in the barter of goods and other various transactions. Tax collectors were notoriously wealthy, most often because they collected more tax than was owed and pocketed the difference. Whether Matthew fits this description at the time Jesus called him will remain a mystery because the Scriptures provide no additional information.

Matthew would have been writing to Jews, however, shown by his appeal to those familiar with Hebrew history. He traces the lineage of Jesus back to Abraham, showing his Jewish heritage. He documents proof that Jesus is the Messiah, who fulfills prophecies of the Old Testament.

Mark, also known as John Mark, is not an apostle though he is well acquainted with them. He is initially a companion of Paul and Barnabas on the first missionary journey, but turns back very early in the journey. This disappoints Paul and eventually becomes a point of disagreement when Paul and Barnabas later determine to visit these same places on the next missionary journey. Barnabas accompanies John Mark on a separate journey from Paul, who chooses to travel with Silas. John Mark, for his part, not only earns the respect of Paul later because of the diligence of his work (2 Tim. 4:11), but is also close to the apostle Peter. Peter considers John Mark to be his "son," a term that doubtless refers to his faith relationship (1 Pet. 5:13).

Mark emphasizes the miracles of Jesus and shows him to be a man who quite literally serves the people. A key verse is Mark 10:45, where Mark quotes Jesus as describing his purpose as being a servant, epitomized by his willingness to go to the cross for the sins of the world.

Luke is called a physician by the apostle Paul (Col. 4:14) and is a person who travels extensively with Paul, perhaps caring for him, on his journeys. As the author of the gospel of Luke and the book of Acts (originally one volume but later separated) Luke frequently indicates his presence on parts of the journeys by inserting "we" in the text when present and referring to the group in third person ("they") when he was absent.

Luke writes to Theophilus with the expressed purpose of giving an orderly account of the events concerning Jesus Christ. With meticulous care and a polished style, he enumerates details of the life of Christ (Gospel of Luke) and the beginning of the church for which Jesus gave His life. His style seems directed to the intellectual and learned Greek audience to show that Jesus was the ideal and universal solution to man's greatest needs.

The author of the Gospel of John is one of the original twelve apostles, known as the apostle of love because of the way he describes himself in the gospel. Instead of self-references as "John" or "I," John chooses to use the phrase, "the disciple whom Jesus loved." As an eyewitness of the events he enumerates, his purpose statement can be found in John 20:30, 31, where he intends to convince readers that Jesus was indeed the Messiah, the son of the living God.

So, the four gospels seem to have four audiences in mind. Matthew seems to be writing for a Jewish audience. Mark seems to be addressing a non-Jewish audience, perhaps more specifically, the Romans. Luke seems to be addressing an intellectual, non-Jewish audience, perhaps the Greeks. And, John emphasizes the deity of Christ as he presents him as "the Son of God."

Omissions in the Accounts

These four accounts of the life of Jesus make no attempt to cover every event in Jesus' life. We have extremely limited information on his childhood with only details of his birth and events surrounding his trip to Jerusalem at the age of 12. Most of the information in the New Testament refers to the time that Jesus began his ministry, which Luke says was at about the age of 30. In writing his gospel, John even makes the statement that "there are also many other things which Jesus did, which if they were written in detail, I suppose that even the world itself would not contain the books which were written" (Jn. 21:25). The limited knowledge we have of Jesus does not mean that Jesus did not have a normal childhood, but rather the writers were emphasizing the relevant activities in His life that have an effect on our beliefs and practice.

The chronology of the events also did not seem to be important to the writers. Lack of clarity on specific events leaves scholars free to speculate on the exact time of the event. For example, in the cleansing of the temple, it is difficult to determine if the event took place at the beginning of his ministry (as Mark and John imply), or at the end of his earthly ministry (as Luke implies). Could this same scenario have occurred twice? These difficulties may never be solved to the satisfaction of every reader. And, the difference does not lessen the effect (or truth) of the text.

In addition, there is no physical description given of Jesus. What makes this most peculiar is that we have physical descriptions of men who lived long before Christ, such as Socrates, Aristotle, and Alexander the Great. But none of Jesus. Again, speculation causes us to wonder if there was a reason that physical descriptions are sparse. Could it have been that God wanted the images of Jesus to be limited to character descriptions and spiritual qualities as opposed to physical characteristics? Certainly we would agree that the spiritual qualities are paramount in our pursuit of Godliness. But the fact remains that very little is said about his physical traits.

Variations in the Four Accounts

When reading each gospel, we see differences in which particular areas the writers emphasize. Luke is the only author of the gospels who mentions that Jesus prayed all night before selecting the Twelve apostles. John is the only writer who describes Jesus' washing the disciples' feet.

In addition, there are several events that seem contradictory. Perhaps the authors were describing similar events, but not the same event, such as two records of the Sermon on the Mount. Perhaps there are contradictions and we are not able to fully understand them because of our lack of understanding of either the original text or actual events taking place in the specific time-period.

The World Into Which Christ Came

There is so much that occurs during the time of the events recorded in the Bible. It is very tempting to view the characters we read about in the Bible in somewhat of a mythical way, that is, never believing that secular events that we might have read about in history occurred simultaneously with the events recorded in the Bible. In addition, the Bible does not claim to be a book of sequential, chronological history nor do the Gospels claim to be biographies. They are documents carefully passed down from generation to generation in order to share the story of God's people. They are primarily best termed 'documents of faith,' or documents upon which early believers and subsequent generations based their beliefs and their hopes.

It would be interesting to speculate as to why Jesus came at the time He did. It might seem to us that it would have been better for Him to come at a time when technology would have helped us more clearly record and preserve specific acts of teaching. Have you ever wondered why it was not possible for us to preserve in some way a means by which we could ascertain what Jesus looked like? Wouldn't it have been wonderful to have audio and/or visual recordings of the Sermon on the Mount or private conversations with believers? In this regard, we must trust the words that Paul spoke to the churches of Galatia when he said, "But when the right time came, God sent His Son" (Gal. 4:4).

What we do know about Jesus' coming is that a period of about 400 years passed between the prophecy of Malachi regarding the coming of the Messiah and the prophecies of John the Baptist, who would announce His coming. Perhaps this is why so many people were attracted to the desert to hear the prophecy of John—there had been such a lack of prophetic messages coming that people were hungering for divine direction. Some believe God wished to dramatize this important event or perhaps the delay was intentionally designed to make it more impressive. While this conclusion is speculative at best, we do know that God was certainly true to His word.

From a variety of sources (i.e., Apocryphal writings, writings of Josephus, a variety of Greek and Roman witnesses, archaeological findings and the Scriptures), we know many of the events that occurred during this 400 year interlude. This time period (425 B.C. – 5 B.C.) would be an excellent subject for study—but it is not the focus of our study together.

To briefly summarize, the times into which the Christ appeared, we know that four empires preceded His coming. The Medo-Persian Period (539-333 B.C.) was followed by the Grecian Period (333-165 B.C.). For students of history, learning of Alexander the Great (333-323 B.C.), the Ptolemies (323-198 B.C.), the Seleucids (198-165 B.C.) provide excellent insight to the culture of the day. The Period of Independence (165-63 B.C.) is followed by the Roman Period (63 B.C. – A.D. 70), providing the desired Divine timeframe for the Savior to be born.

Looking back from our perspective, we can see that several key events transpired that would have made this an ideal time. The Romans had achieved the *Pax Romana*, a time of relative peace in the land so that travel could be extended and communication over great distances was possible. They had also developed an extensive system of roads which allowed easier travel. The Greek language had become the language of commerce and so there was an excellent means of taking specific and accurate messages to a wide variety of people. Perhaps these might be some of the reasons that this time was chosen. The time for the coming of the Messiah had also been predicted to be in the days of the Roman kings by the prophet Daniel (Dan. 2:44). So, regardless of our reasoning and justification, it was providential that Christ would come when He did and in the manner in which He came.

Important Facts About Jesus As the Christ

Jesus in Prophecy

We do know about Jesus as the fulfillment of the promise for a Messiah when we read the Old and New Testaments. This is a crucial step and one that is taken for granted by those of us living in the 21st century. Had we been living in the 1st century, it would have been very difficult for many of us to accept that Jesus was the promised Messiah for several reasons. Primarily, the Jews were looking for a Messiah that would bring Israel back to national prominence. Their expectation was not for a quiet man of humble lineage to come in and work in such a way so as not to call attention to himself. They expected a mighty leader, perhaps with soldiers, quite possibly with priestly credentials to redeem Israel. For Jesus to come from such obscurity and make such audacious claims certainly aroused suspicion and doubt among the religious leaders. For this redeemer to allow himself to be crucified was the final form of proof needed to show that he was an imposter.

To say that any honest Jew would have readily accepted Jesus as the Messiah is a vicious and indefensible charge. Saul of Tarsus was a leading Jew, a Pharisee nonetheless, and he was not convinced that Jesus was the Christ until he experienced the miraculous vision on the road to Damascus. Once convinced, he became a tireless and selfless worker for the cause of Christ. Others believed once they weighed the evidence, including the study of the Law and the witnessing of the miracles.

From the perspective of the 21st century, however, we are able to compare Scriptures and see that Jesus did indeed meet the qualifications so established by prophets of old and confirmed by New Testament witnesses. Read the following Scriptures and you can see the evidence that seems so obvious to a Bible-believer now. Remember as you read, however, that those living in the 1st century did not have all the evidence that we now have in our possession.

Remember two things as we progress: (1) we must see for ourselves what the Bible says in order to learn these important truths, and (2) there is no substitute for opening up our Bibles and reading. You will be amazed at how your knowledge of God will grow and your faith in Him will increase as you spend time with the Scriptures.

Remember, we are focusing on Christ. The Bible predicts that a Messiah (a savior) will come. Jesus uniquely fits every prophecy in the Old Testament regarding the coming Messiah.

One of the most convicting proofs of the truths of the Bible is its predictive nature. We read in the Old Testament of something that will take place in the future and then we read of its actually occurring in the New Testament. The predictive nature of the Bible is a part of the proof of its truth.

The Old Testament Tells of Jesus

Jesus was alive at the beginning of the creation (Gen. 1:26; Heb. 1:1, 2).

Jesus described himself as the "I am," a term used by God to describe himself to Moses, and a statement used by Jesus which astounded and confounded the Jews listening to him (Ex. 3:14; John 8:58).

The reason for the first prophecy was to reveal that there was 'good news' for those that needed deliverance from the consequences of sin (Gen. 3:15).

Moses prophesied that the Jews should one day listen to a prophet that would come from their own countrymen (Deut. 18:15-19).

Matthew connects a prophecy of the coming Messiah (Isa. 7:14) with the birth of Jesus (Mt. 1:22-25).

The Old Testament closes with the prophecy of John the Baptist who will usher in the Messiah (Mal. 4:5, 6).

The prophecy of the coming of John the Baptist and Jesus is said to have been fulfilled in the New Testament (Jn. 1:19-27; Mt. 11:14).

The story of the 'suffering servant' is a script for the life of Jesus (Isa. 53).

A specific time for the appearance of the kingdom is given by Daniel— in the days of the Roman kings (Dan. 2:31-45).

The Child Jesus

We read in the Gospels of the childhood of Jesus. We don't read many details, not nearly as many as we desire, but the picture that we read is sufficient to give us an indication of a life that was fairly typical of a Jewish boy up until the time that he began his ministry.

Jesus' birth was special because he was born to a young virgin named Mary. He was conceived by the Holy Spirit (Lk. 1:26-31).

Jesus was born in Bethelehem (Lk. 2:4-7).

King Herod learned that a king was born in Bethlehem, and he became highly suspicious (Mt. 2:1-3).

Jesus had at least four brothers and at least two sisters (Mk. 6:3).

He received a well-rounded childhood, evidenced by growth in four areas. He grew intellectually, physically, spiritually and socially (Lk. 2:41-52).

Jesus grew up in the home of a carpenter, Joseph (Mt. 13:55).

Jesus at 12 years old astounded the teachers in the temple with His knowledge and understanding (Jn. 2:46-48).

Jesus began his ministry when he was about 30 years of age (Lk. 3:23).

Jesus is Tempted

When we learn of Jesus, we learn of a person was fully human and fully divine. This is wonderful news because we learn that Jesus knows all about the temptations that we will face. Many texts of Scripture are useful for teaching us about these temptations.

Temptation is defined as being drawn away because of our own individual desires (James 1:12).

Jesus was led into the wilderness for the express purpose of being tempted by Satan (Mt. 4:1).

We know that God is not tempted with sin and does not tempt man with sin (James 1:13). This is also helpful in understanding how Jesus could be God and man. He was not tempted as God but rather as a man.

One of the occurrences that added to the temptation of Jesus was that he had been fasting for 40 days and nights and was hungry (Mt. 4:2).

The apostle John describes the three sources of appeal in temptation when he states that we are drawn to the world by the (1) lust of the eyes (2) lust of the flesh and (3) the pride of life (1 Jn. 2:15-17).

Jesus helps us understand how to handle temptation by showing us how he handled his temptations from Satan. He relied on the Scriptures and referred to it in time of temptation (Mt. 4:4, 7, 10).

When Jesus refused to give in to Satan, the devil left him for a time (Mt. 4:11).

We are comforted in temptation because we see that Jesus did not lash out in anger or revenge, but rather entrusted himself to God the Father and relied upon him for strength (1 Pet. 2:21-23).

Jesus had an advantage over Satan because he was knowledgeable of his ways and schemes (2 Cor. 2:11).

One blessing we have that should help us during temptation is the fact that God has full control over our temptation and will not allow us to be tempted above our level of strength. He promises to always provide a way of escape (1 Cor. 10:13).

Jesus Chooses His Apostles

Now Jesus has officially started his ministry. He is purposefully walking among the people, and it isn't long until we see what he has in mind.

Jesus prayed all night before he called his disciples to him and chose twelve of them to be his apostles (Lk. 6:12-13).

The apostles' personalities were starkly distinct. A character study of the twelve shows they are extreme opposites in personality. Their devotion to the Lord is noteworthy (Lk. 6:14-16).

There was one man, Paul, who was called as an apostle at a later time. He was not one of the original twelve but had a unique ministry, evidenced by the work of God in his life (1 Cor. 1:1; 15:8).

Paul came to be an apostle by a special call from Jesus Christ (Gal. 1:1).

His specific mission was to take the Gospel to the Gentiles (Rom. 15:15-16).

We could spend so much time just discussing the selection and training of the apostles themselves. Jesus spent a significant amount of time with these 12 men when they had only a partial conception of what Jesus had in mind. They simply knew that they believed he was the Messiah and they were intent on following him, even to the point of death. Indications are that they anticipated an earthly kingdom, but as the time for his sacrificial death on the cross approached, Jesus would begin to be more specific in his private conversations about what was to take place.

I am encouraged by the fact that even though these men did not know everything that the coming of Jesus entailed, they were faithful to the cause and open to his corrective teaching. One, of course, would ultimately betray Jesus. Jesus seems to have been aware of the impending betrayal from the beginning.

The Painful Experiences in Jerusalem

Finally the time comes when Jesus' ministry has been completed, and he moves toward Jerusalem for the last time. The time was so brief, perhaps 2 ½ to 3 years. But in that time, he had accomplished everything necessary for his kingdom to come to fruition and for the apostles to lead the faithful to a glorious ministry.

Notice the innocence of Jesus and the pressure under which Pilate made his decision to convict him. As you read the accounts, you'll be reminded of the audacious statements made about the Son of God and the willpower necessary for Jesus not to obliterate all those who were falsely accusing him. Since God cannot co-exist with sin, how much endurance must it have required of him not to do away with his false accusers?

Each of the Gospels describes the series of events from the trial through the resurrection in unique ways. The same events are described in subtly distinctive ways.

Matthew views Jesus as the Messiah because he was writing to a Jewish audience. He vividly describes the betrayal, arrest and trial of Jesus with great attention to the disrespect that Jesus received from the Jews.

Mark describes the events leading up to the crucifixion with great attention to the progression of events. He numbers the days, more clearly showing the last week of Jesus' life than the other writers. His description has a dark tone and focuses on the dramatic presentation of who Jesus was.

Luke, the physician, surprisingly gives less description of the physical experience of enduring a crucifixion. His brief description of the crucifixion is summed up in one phrase, "And when they came to the place called The Skull, there they crucified him and the criminals, one on the right and the other on the left." Perhaps we would be expecting more regarding the physical side, but Luke is insistent on giving an orderly account of events that transpired.

John picks up on stories and perspectives the other Gospel writers have left out. Since his purpose is to convince his readers that Jesus is the Christ (Jn. 20:30-31), he tells stories that emphasize the response of people to the fact of the crucifixion.

Each of the accounts shows a different perspective on the suffering of Jesus. We come away from these stories with a renewed sense of amazement at the extent to which Jesus went to give the appropriate sacrifice to save mankind.

The Resurrection of Jesus

We should be careful not to overlook the response of initial shock and disbelief on the part of those realizing Jesus had been raised. Little wonder as to why people would have been shocked. Perhaps those who believed that Jesus was the Messiah never did expect him to be killed in the first place. After all, here was a man who could heal the sick, cast out demons, raise the dead, miraculously produce food to feed thousands, and control the wind and the rain. How could he allow someone to take his life?

Once his life was taken, you can imagine the disbelief at hearing that he was dead, only to be followed by extreme joy and exaltation in the fact that he had been raised from the dead. What a roller-coaster of emotions!

The Second Coming

The next event on the horizon for the world is the second coming of Christ. We know from the Scriptures that Jesus came the first time to this world to give his life as a ransom for the sins of mankind. He will come the second time to receive the faithful into his presence forever.

We should not forget that Jesus said he was going to prepare a place and would come back for his children to be with them forever (Jn. 14:2-3).

We will know when Jesus comes because every eye will see him when he comes in the sky (Rev. 1:7).

One thing we know for sure is that we do not know for sure when he is coming (Mt. 24:42-43).

Those Christians who are alive at his coming will have their bodies transformed instantaneously from a physical body (mortal) to a spiritual body (immortal) (1 Cor. 15:51-53).

When the Lord comes in the sky, those Christians who have died will come with the Lord in the air (1 Thess. 4:16).

When the Lord comes again, this earth and all the elements of the earth will burn away with a fervent heat (2 Pet. 3:10-11).

Our Responsibility

The Bible is fairly specific when it speaks of the second coming. There are specific issues mentioned in great detail. However, the emphasis in the Bible does not seem to be on the eternal reward or punishment as it does on the responsibility of God's people to live faithfully while still on the earth.

The Bible teaches us that there is only one resurrection. Those who are faithful will have the resurrection of life. Those who have not believed and committed evil deeds will have the resurrection of judgment (Jn. 5:28-29).

The Bible also graphically depicts the judgment scene when all of mankind will stand before the judgment seat in order to receive the pronouncement of reward or punishment (Mt. 25:31-36). The Bible's explicit description of Hell makes it a place that is repugnant to the serious thinker (Rev. 21:8).

The importance of knowing the life of Christ is not just an academic exercise. It impacts each of our lives on a physical and spiritual level. We live for the Lord on earth because our desire is to live with the Lord for eternity.

Chapter 6 · *What You Should Know...*

- the definition of sin
- four ways the Scripture states that we sin
- the example in Romans of man's struggle with sin
- answers to seven critical questions regarding salvation.

7   THE STUDY OF SALVATION

Soteriology

Before anyone begins a trip to a new location, they usually consult a map. Even if you are using the latest technology to find your way, you'll need to enter your starting place. Let's begin by seeing where you are.

If I were seated next to you, I would want to ask certain questions. I would hope that you wouldn't be offended by my asking you privately, but each of us would probably have a different response. I would hope that you would answer them honestly before you read on.

First of all, *would you consider yourself to be a part of a religious group or organization at the present time?* It really doesn't matter at this point what the group is or what they believe. The question is whether you consider yourself to be a part of it.

Second, *what is the name of the group*, and how much do you know about it? Is it a local group, or does it have national or international connections?

Third, *can you identify one specific time when you made a commitment to Christ?* However you define 'making a commitment,' try to describe the situation around the moment. What happened that led you to believe that this was a significant moment?

How old were you at the time? Were you old enough to describe the moment on your own?

Have you ever been baptized? Perhaps it was not necessary for you to be baptized during this moment of commitment to Christ. But consider: Have you been baptized at any time since your moment of commitment?

Many religious people make a confession sometime during their spiritual experience. A confession is a statement of belief—an admittance to certain beliefs or convictions. Did you make a confession at that time?

Were you saved before or after you were baptized? This is a key question that you must answer before we move on. Think seriously about it, and then jot yourself a note explaining your answer.

Great! Now that we have that accomplished, we can begin to see where God intends for us to be. This is an exciting study—even though it covers so much ground—because we will literally be looking at passages in the Bible ranging from the first book to the last.

The very use of the word salvation can be very confusing. The story of salvation has to begin with a story of something that is lost. You might be surprised at the answer you would receive if you were to ask someone, "Are you lost?" The obvious response would be, "No, I'm not lost. I know exactly where I am." And, of course, they would be thinking about being lost physically as opposed to spiritually. So, there must be an understanding of what the Bible means by saying we are lost.

In Genesis 3, the story of the sin of Adam and Eve is told. It's a simple story, really. A story of a serpent that is able to talk and deceive Eve into believing the command she has received is not only untrue but not in her best interest. She is told that even though she was instructed not to eat of the tree of knowledge of good and evil, she should understand that true knowledge and the ability to become like God would come only if she ate of the fruit of this tree. She, unfortunately, eats of the fruit and gives some to Adam and he eats it. This is a sin because it was an act of defiance against God. They were told what to do—they understood it—and they deliberately acted in a contrary manner. Therefore, they must pay the consequences.

When we read Genesis 3, however, we not only see the curse pronounced against the woman and the man—but also against the serpent (who is identified as Satan in Revelation 12:9). There is, however, a slight indication in that curse that the serpent may "bruise him (the seed of woman) on the heel," but that the seed of woman (referenced as God [Christ] in Rom. 16:20) would ultimately crush the head of the serpent. Some have called this the *protoeuangelion*, which is the Greek equivalent of 'first gospel.' This gives hope to all generations since Adam that God has a plan to 'redeem,' or buy back man from the guilt of his sins.

God Reveals His Plan for Redemption

Keep reading in your Old Testament, and you'll come to Genesis 12, where God speaks to Abram (later called Abraham) and gives him a sevenfold promise of reward. He commands Abram to go from his own country to a place that He will show him. Abram is obedient, and God gives him a sevenfold blessing in return, which is enumerated in Genesis 12:1-3. They are:

1. "I will make you a great nation"
2. "I will bless you"
3. "I will make your name great"
4. "You shall be a blessing"
5. "I will bless those who bless you"
6. "The one who curses you will be cursed"
7. "You will bless all the families of the earth"

When Abram obeyed God, God was faithful to His promises. This is an important principle that follows to this day. We may not need to go to a distant land where we have never been, but God does require that we obey His commands without knowing the process by which he will achieve His will in our lives.

As we continue to read in the Old Testament, we see that God doesn't leave the Jews without a knowledge of His will. The entirety of the Old Testament is filled with passages enumerating the specific requirements of God. The reason for the command may not always be given but the point that God expected these commands to be obeyed should not be overlooked.

At times, the commands were very specific. For example, the book of Leviticus is filled with instructions for the people to have and maintain a healthy relationship with God. Even a casual reader of this book would be impressed by its attention to detail. The first 7 chapters list the sins that man commits and the accompanying sacrifice required by God for reconciliation. The practice of sacrifices did not originate with the book of Leviticus (for example, read Ex. 5:1-3; 18:12; 24:5), but the people did receive instruction on what type of sacrifices were necessary to address particular sins. There were burnt offerings, grain offerings, peace offerings, sin offerings and guilt offerings discussed in the first seven chapters. A summary statement is found in Lev. 7:37, 38 that emphasizes God's expectations.

These expectations were serious and severe. For example, homosexuality is addressed in Lev. 18:22 and 20:13. It would be difficult to say that the Bible never addresses the topic of homosexuality or 'same-sex attraction.' In fact, the apostle Paul addresses it in the New Testament in several places (Rom. 1:27; 1 Cor. 6:9). Here, as in other places, there are expectations of obedience to the will of God.

God's Plan for Sharing the Message

It isn't enough to know that God has a plan. We must know how to learn his desires so that we are able to pass it down to succeeding generations. Through this process of God revealing his will (divine revelation) we are able to see how God could hold us accountable for obedience.

The book of Deuteronomy is a book filled with the sermons of Moses, who recounts the will of God for the benefit of the Jews. In Deuteronomy 6, he gives instructions to parents—who are to develop their faith and then systematically pass that down to their children at every available opportunity. Part of this instruction is still repeated when Jews gather as they still recite the *Shema* (pronounced sheh-mah') in their religious services. The word *shema* is the Hebrew word for 'listen' or 'hear.' We sometimes even sing it in our devotional and worship services as we remember the words of Jesus when he reminded us of the responsibilities inherent in this simple prayer (Mt. 22:37).

But the main idea is that God expected parents to learn His will and then teach His will to their children. The family was the primary place for training and instruction. Unfortunately, as families struggle for survival and parents are no longer living up to their responsibility, our children are the ones suffering by not learning the truths of the Bible or their responsibility to obey God's commands. That does not mean we do not have children who want to do what is right. It does mean that children are not always learning correctly the difference between right and wrong.

The Bible also teaches that we are individually accountable for obedience. Some would like to believe that we can blame our parents, or our government, or our educational institutions for the mistakes that we make. However, we read differently in the Bible.

The prophet Ezekiel tells a proverb given to him by God (and recorded in Ezekiel 18) in which God shows that each person is responsible for his own sin. Ezekiel relates a message from God in which a man lives who is very righteous but has a son who is guilty of violence, robbery, adultery and other specific heinous acts. This son has a son of his own who is very righteous. God teaches us that the son is not guilty for the sins of the father, and by implication, the son does not inherit the righteousness of his father. Each man is held accountable for his own actions.

This same principle is carried over into the teachings of the New Testament. As an example, Jesus is quoted by John as teaching that the type of resurrection people experience, whether a resurrection of life or a resurrection of punishment, is directly related to their actions in life. Each person is held accountable for his own actions.

You are probably thinking, if not saying, "Why are we spending so much time in the Old Testament when you stated in earlier chapters that we are living under a new law? Where does Christianity come in?" And I would say, "Good question. Let's look at a specific New Testament passage that seems to contain all the elements we need to know for learning about salvation."

God's Messianic Plan Revealed

Messianic plan is another way of saying that God had, from the beginning (at least from the Garden of Eden and arguably from the beginning of creation), planned for a Messiah to come to rescue man from his lost condition.

It seems to me to be an obvious choice to look at the opening chapters of the book of Acts to see God's plan in full display. This passage is an obvious choice for several reasons. First, it represents the place at which the church, promised earlier by Jesus when he spoke with the apostles in Caesarea Philippi (Mt.16), comes to fruition. It also comes after we read the gospels which tell of the life of Jesus—but do not tell how to 'be added to the Lord's church.' It is important to remember that Jesus was focusing his attention on the Jews while he lived on the earth, and he was laboring to get them to receive him as the promised Messiah. But more about that later.

You'll have to get your own Bible as we read the first two chapters of the book of Acts. As you read, please note the section of the text that I will identify. As you read the biblical text, fill in the blanks on the questions that I will ask—just so that we don't miss anything.

Let's begin with Acts 1:1-4. Jesus spends his time with a specific group of people. This group is the apostles. We can see this at the end of Acts 1:2 and the beginning of the next verse. In this chapter, we read of Jesus talking with the disciples for a period of about 40 days "speaking of the things concerning the kingdom of God." This was the focus of his teaching. But remember, the group he is addressing in these first two chapters will specifically be the apostles.

In Acts 1:5-8, Jesus promises that the Holy Spirit will come upon them (the apostles) with power. We should notice that this was promised to them. They were not commanded to be baptized in the Holy Spirit. They were told that the Holy Spirit would come upon them. No one is ever told in the Bible to be baptized in the Holy Spirit.

We should probably notice that there are specific qualifications given for those men that were called apostles in the Bible. The literal definition of the word apostle is "one sent." So, in one sense, an apostle would be any one who is sent on a journey or mission, etc. But in the Bible, there is a specific group of individuals that are called the apostles of Jesus that were chosen by him for a specific task. He chooses this select group (Mt. 10:2-4; Mk. 3:16-19; Lk. 6:14-16) from among his followers and invests much of his time training them. The Bible specifically calls them the apostles, or the Twelve. This is always understood to be these 12 men chosen by Jesus.

But when Judas betrays the Lord and subsequently takes his own life, the apostles know that his position among the twelve had to be replaced. This is detailed in Acts 1 where Peter stands up and quotes from the Psalms and expresses the need for filling his office. Now the task of finding another apostle is brought into view. Peter gives the qualifications of the men who would be candidates in Acts 1:21-22. The two qualifications he mentions are (1) the person must have seen the Lord and (2) the person must have been with the Lord from his baptism until his ascension. They choose two men from whom God would indicate his choice as the next apostle. Matthias is chosen and he joins the apostles in their continued work.

This might be the best time to pause and notice that there is not a man alive today who could meet the qualifications for an apostle as set out by Peter in Acts 1. There may be great followers of the Lord and even great leaders for the Lord. But there are no modern-day apostles in the sense of the original twelve, with either their authority or their power, because there are no men who could meet the qualifications that are listed.

Acts 1 and Acts 2 are frequently thought of as different chapters, but since man has devised these divisions of chapters and verses, the storyline of Luke actually continues through the book as though no division existed. In other words, chapters one and two continue to have the apostles as the subject of the activities. In Acts 2:1, when the Bible says, "And when the day of Pentecost has come, they were all together in one place," the pronoun "they" actually refers to the twelve apostles. This is critical because the Holy Spirit would come upon them (the apostles) just as they (the apostles) had been promised in Acts 1:8. It was not the entire group in Jerusalem that received this power from God, but rather these apostles.

Feel free to read the rest of the chapter, but remember that we come back later to look at the activities mentioned by the coming of the Holy Spirit in Chapter 9. For now, notice that Peter stands up and begins preaching to the Jews. His sermon is wonderful. It is simple. It is scriptural. It is Christ-centered. He tells them that they had all seen Jesus, had witnessed the miracles, and had put him to death on the cross. He continued by saying that God raised him from the dead, and they had all seen his resurrection (Acts 2:32).

The group that Peter was addressing was the Jewish crowd in Jerusalem on the Day of Pentecost. The city would have been bustling with Jewish people in and around the Temple. Peter was preaching a sermon that literally convicted them of having crucified the Son of God—the very man who was currently seated at the right hand of God (Acts 2:33).

Peter preached this sermon so effectively that when he finished (at the end of verse 36), the listeners are 'pierced to the heart' and ask the apostles, "Brethren, what shall we do?" Notice his answer. It was not vague or equivocal. He gave two specific actions that they were to do in order to be obedient.

They were told to repent and be baptized for the forgiveness of sins.

Please notice that they were not told simply to believe and trust in the Lord for forgiveness. Nor were they told to believe and say a prayer in order to be forgiven. They already believed that Jesus was the Christ or they wouldn't have asked the question. Since they believed, Peter told them to repent (make a change in their lives) and be baptized (immersed into water) for the forgiveness of sins and to receive the gift of the Holy Spirit.

This is such an important place in redemptive history. I know there are several key times in history—each worthy of pausing and giving thanks. What a significant time the birth of Jesus was—a time that would never be repeated. What a significant time the crucifixion was—that time in history when the sinless son of God took upon himself the sins of all mankind. Of course, who could forget the resurrection of Jesus from the dead? Peter used this very incident as the driving force of the sermon.

But here, in Acts 2, Peter is announcing the method by which an individual could receive both the forgiveness of sin and the gift of the Holy Spirit in the same act. John the Baptist had been preaching a baptism for the forgiveness of sins (Mk. 1:4), but the baptism of John the Baptist did not bring with it the gift of the Spirit. This is clearly shown in Acts 19, when twelve men from Ephesus, (who had been baptized in John's baptism) learned about the baptism taught by Peter. It is significant that these men knew that there was a specific reason why a person was baptized. The Jews in Jerusalem would have been very familiar with baptisms and washings taught in the Old Testament as a way of becoming ceremonially clean in the sight of God (Heb. 9:8-11). But here, Peter was telling them how they might receive forgiveness and the gift of the Spirit by their simple obedience. This obedience required repentance and baptism in the name of Jesus Christ.

Peter continues to exhort (encourage) them to act quickly. In fact, verse 40 states that he uses many other words, solemnly testifying to them so that they would "be saved from this untoward (perverse) generation." This shows clearly that before they complied with the command stated in verse 38, they were in a "lost" condition. Salvation deals with the idea of saving someone who is lost.

If you believe the Bible to be true, then when these people were obedient to the command, that is, when they repented and were baptized in the name of Jesus Christ, they received forgiveness of sins and the gift of the Holy Spirit. This chapter tells us that 3,000 people were baptized into Christ on that day. One of the reasons that so many would have been baptized is that these Jews were very familiar with the concept of a coming Messiah. They had just never envisioned this carpenter and executed rabbi to be Jesus of Nazareth. When they learned that the very one they had witnessed being crucified was the one to not only come back from the grave, but also to be the fulfillment of the Scriptures' prophecies, they were not hesitant to respond.

Another reason that 3,000 would be baptized here is that they had never before been told that this baptism was a part of the plan of God. Peter had the privilege of being the first to announce the method by which individuals could be ushered into the family of God. This was a fulfillment of what was told him when Jesus said to Peter, "I will give you the keys of the kingdom of heaven; and whatever you shall bind on earth shall have been bound in heaven, and whatever you shall loose on earth shall have been loosed in heaven" (Mt. 16:19). This doesn't mean Peter saves us. It means that Peter was the first to announce God's plan for the redemption of man.

When these people were baptized, they were added to family of God, the church. It is still true today. This message has not changed.

A person doesn't just join a church like we would join a Civitan Club or Kiwanis Club. Once a person submits to the will of God, which means obedience to His will, the Lord adds that person to the church (Acts 2:47). The Bible speaks of only one church—but we'll talk about that later (Chapters 10 and 11).

This is a time to pause and prayerfully reflect on what we have learned from the first two chapters in the book of Acts.

Is the Bible the authoritative will of God? If I believe the Bible to be true, then I can believe that the same promises made to believers in the first century are the same promises made to those that lived many years after (Acts 2:39). If I don't believe the Bible to be true, then I can believe and practice anything I like. But I should not expect to receive the promises listed in the Bible either.

In other words, this passage teaches that those who were obedient received forgiveness of sins and the gift of the Spirit. At the same time, it implies that those who were not obedient did not receive either gift that was promised to the obedient. No repentance and baptism? No forgiveness of sins and no gift of the Spirit.

Now, let me ask you an important question. Were they saved before or after they were baptized?

Let's re-read Acts 2:38. Peter said, "Repent and let each of you be baptized in the name of Jesus Christ for the forgiveness of your sins; and you shall receive the gift of the Holy Spirit." Why were they baptized? In order to receive these two promises. When did the forgiveness come? After the repentance and baptism. When was the gift given? After repentance and baptism.

Some believe that a person is baptized because his sins have already been forgiven. They understand the word translated "for" to also mean "on account of." In some cases, it does. However compare a passage that uses the exact same construction and see what the result would be.

In Matthew's gospel, we read of Jesus meeting with his apostles, introducing the concept of the Lords supper. It was at the time when they were celebrating the Passover. He took some of the bread which would have been a part of their meal, gave thanks, and gave it to his disciples. He then took a cup of wine, gave a blessing, and distributed it to each of his disciples. And when he distributed the cup of wine, he said, "Drink from it, all of you; for this is my blood of the covenant, which is to be shed on behalf of many for forgiveness of sins" (Mt. 26:27, 28). It is the same construction as in Acts 2:38. This act is for forgiveness of sins.

Is this act 'for,' (in order to receive) forgiveness of sins, or 'for '(on account of) forgiveness of sins? If it means because your sins are already forgiven (on account of), then Jesus would be saying, 'my blood will be shed because your sins are already forgiven.' The forgiveness of sins would precede his death on the cross. There would have been no need for Jesus to go to the cross. But, of course, the only way sins can be forgiven is by the shedding of the blood of the sinless son of God (Heb. 9:11-14). Had Jesus not gone to the cross, we would still be living with our sins.

The significance of baptism is not a type of 'magic in the water.' It is not the location of the water, whether it is a river or pool. It is the act of submission to the will of God that represents the final state at which a person is forgiven of his sins, receives the gift of the Holy Spirit, and is added to the body of Christ. The Bible is telling us to submit to the will of God by submitting to baptism (the word literally means immersion, dipping, or plunging) in the name of (by the authority of) Jesus Christ. It is a baptism into Jesus Christ.

This is such an important part of our study in this book. The Bible teaches us Jesus came to live a perfect life on this earth and to give it as a ransom for our souls. The only method by which man can receive forgiveness of sin in his life is by making contact with the blood of Christ. Obedience to the will of God is the only way. When we believe in Jesus, repent of our sins, confess Jesus as Lord, and are baptized into the name of Jesus Christ, we receive the forgiveness of our sins. We honor God by obeying his word.

Chapter 7 · *What You Should Know...*

- a 'pre-test'—positions prior to study of specific scriptures
- God's call to Abraham in Genesis 12
- God's plan for sharing the message (Dt. 6)
- events on Day of Pentecost as described in Acts 2
- answers to specific questions regarding obedience.

8   THE STUDY OF ANGELS

Angels, Demons, and Satan

I don't know of a topic that stirs as much interest as the subject of angels and demons. I suppose this great interest in the subject is warranted for several reasons with which you may find yourself in agreement or in violent opposition. But I maintain that our interest is as varied as our personalities, predispositions, and experience.

Subjects that are 'mysterious' have always been especially appealing. By that I mean that there is so much that is unknown about angels and demons that any fragment of alleged evidence that might prove their existence is tantalizingly attractive. For example, it would be wonderfully exciting to think that mysterious forces for good are at work that ultimately eliminate and overpower any negative action on my part so as to bring about beneficial results. It would be the 'trump card' that would subsequently and sequentially 'cancel' any poor move made by a human being. To think that this is accomplished secretly and silently adds to the intrigue.

On the other hand, what would it be to consider the work of demons? These sinister forces would be considered as works of an adversary who is not content with confusion and chaos in our lives, but rather the total destruction of the 'spiritual man' within us. Could it be that these sinister forces can 'overpower' our best intentions to bring about evil consequences even for the one who has the best of intentions? Can we know?

How do we respond? The only viable means possible is to understand that the only reliable source for information on the existence of angels and demons is the Bible. We should and we will explore the books of the Old and New Testaments in order to determine our response.

So much could be said about this topic, but since this is a general review of what the Bible says about angels, I will simply make a statement about the facts found in the Bible and an accompanying text in which more could be gleaned. It should be noted that some of these issues are still keenly debated among Bible students and scholars. Without apology, I will try to stay to the main issues and briefly identify areas that would be worth more biblical investigation.

Angels

From the Bible, we know the following:

Angels, Scripture tells us, exist. Though there is much about them that is shrouded in mystery, we know they exist because they are spoken of as having been in existence at the time of the creation of the world (Job 38:7). Though we know they were not always in existence, but rather were created by God, through Jesus Christ, at a time prior to the creation of the world.

As observed in Psalms 148: 2, 5: *Praise him, all his angels, praise him, all his heavenly hosts…Let them praise the name of the Lord, for he commanded and they were created.*

Angels are spirits. We read frequently in Scriptures that angels can take the form of human beings, but they are spiritual beings that transcend physical limitations (Ps. 104:4.)

Angels can be good or bad. Jesus spoke of the "devil and his angels" (Mt. 25:41), so we should be careful not to assume that 'being angelic' always refers to virtuous qualities.

Angels fulfill a certain function. By definition, angels (from the Greek word, *angelos*) are messengers. They carry and deliver the messages given to them by God.

Angels minister to us (Heb. 1:14). Since we know that angels exist and minister to us, it stands to reason that they are very interested in us. Jesus tells of rejoicing in Heaven in the presence of angels when a sinner repents of sin and comes back to God (Lk. 15:7).

Angels are directly accountable to God. Some have even been disobedient and have received punishment (2 Pet. 2:4, Rev. 20:1-3). Since the word angel by definition means messenger, the angel is responsible for effectively carrying out divine desires.

Angels are created beings. Jesus told the Sadducees (Mt. 22:30) that marriage will not be an occurrence in Heaven, but rather that the souls of men would be like the angels, who do not marry. Angels would then be asexual beings who do not procreate—they do not mate and produce infant angels.

Angels are subdivided into various categories—perhaps even a hierarchy of angels. For example, the Bible mentions in Exodus 25 that Cherubim (plural of cherub) were to be put in the tabernacle of the Jews. In addition, Gabriel and Michael are both named archangels. Exactly how that differs from Seraphim and Cherubim is uncertain, but there seems to be a definite hierarchy among angels, perhaps even extending to evil angels.

Angels are described as being of a higher order than man but a lower order than God. The Psalms contain a reference to the fact that man "was made for a little while lower than the angels" (Ps. 8:4 and Heb. 2:6-8) so there seems to be a differentiation between the two groups.

Angels can be invisible but can be made visible when allowed by God. Genesis 18 mentions that three men come to Abraham to discuss future events and eventually the conversation is referred to as a conversation between Abraham and "the Lord," which implies a revelation of God coming from these men. Genesis 19 mentions that "two angels" appear to Lot and the men of the city call for "the men" to be delivered to them, so they must have had the appearance of men. Even Satan himself is described as being able to "disguise himself as an angel of light" (2 Cor. 11:14). These events are shrouded in mystery and are yet fascinating in understanding God's use of angels.

Angels can assume any one of a number of forms. They have been seen in the form of horses (2 Sam. 6:14-17), or winds (Heb. 1:7), or as flames of fire.

Angels have superhuman knowledge, but they are not omniscient. By definition, angels are given specific messages that they are able to communicate to chosen humans. Peter writes that there are some things that angels desired to know, implying the limitations of their knowledge (1 Pet. 1:12).

Angels have superhuman power. One angel killed 185,000 soldiers (2 Kgs. 19:35), and Michael decided to defer to the power of God in dealing with Satan (Jude 9). Numerous other passages refer to the mighty spiritual battles that occur.

There are innumerable angels—too many to count. We read of various descriptions of the numbers. Myriads (myriad equals 10,000) of angels are described in Heaven and sometimes "myriads of myriads" (Rev. 5:11).

Angels are not to be worshiped. The Hebrew writer specifically warns against worshiping angels (Heb. 1:1-14). Angels are servants that serve the Lord, the only one worthy of worship.

Demons

There are several views regarding the origin of demons. Unfortunately, we do not have time to explore each view, but you should be aware that these views exist and cause us to go back to the Scriptures to verify their validity. For example, the following beliefs do have adherents, though I do not believe them to be supported by Scripture.

Some believe that demons are believed to be the spirits of evil men who lived in times past and now take up residence in other men. Others speculate that demons are believed to be the disembodied spirits of the 'nephilim' of Genesis 6:1ff. These would be the evil spirits of spiritual beings that cohabited with man. Another group believes that demons belong to a race of people who lived on earth before Adam and that the demons were disembodied spirits of those men (Gen. 1:1, 2). Still others believe that demons are fallen angels—with Satan or Beelzebub (Jesus uses these terms interchangeably) as the prince of demons (Mt. 12:24-29; Mk. 3:22-26). Time prohibits a full discussion of each of these theories, weighing the strengths and weaknesses of each position. Needless to say, I believe the answer to be something other than the conclusions that have been drawn.

Even though these perspectives are highly speculative, the fact is undeniable that *the Bible speaks of the reality of demons.* Eighty New Testament references to 'devils,' 'spirits,' 'unclean spirits,' 'foul spirits,' and 'evil spirits.' In fact, Jesus spent a significant amount of His time on earth with the demon possessed (Mk. 1:34).

Frequently, demons have been dismissed as something explainable. They have been called maniacs or those with a mental illness (Mt. 4:24 seems to show a distinction made between the two).

Another popular means of explaining demons in the Bible is to ascribe reasons for Jesus using these stories. Some ascribe it to an accommodation theory, where Jesus took a very popular belief of His day and used it in His teaching, thus accommodating Himself to the thinking of the time. Or perhaps it was limitationism, in which Jesus was a 'child of his time,' and as such, thought that demons were real. His knowledge was limited and sometimes erroneous, this theory says.

What we do know is that the Bible speaks of demons as principally a New Testament phenomenon. The activity of demons begins to taper off immediately after the ministry of Jesus.

Regardless, *there are some things we know about demons*. First of all, they are fascinating. Simply thinking about demons taking control of a person's life in the first century can be intriguing. How could a demon control someone's life?

We also know that they were and are real (not just a sickness—Mt. 4:24). Even though they do not take control of *our* lives (the subject of which concept requires another entire chapter yet to be written), they were and are very powerful (Mt. 9:32; Mt. 12:22; Mk. 5).

We do know that they were active during Jesus' time in unusual ways. For example, no Old Testament passages refer to demon possessions, but that does not mean that there are not plenty of examples of demons. Additionally, there is no mention in the writings of the New Testament as to how one should guard against demon possession. (Demon possession is distinct from being considered as being tempted by the Devil). The people who were demon possessed were never chastised for being possessed, nor were they ever told to repent.

The Bible also reflects a definite relationship between God (Christ) and Demons. Mark 5 seems to be an excellent focal point for study to see this relationship.

The Scriptures teach that demons recognized and knew Jesus (Mk. 5:6, 7). They called Jesus the "Son of the Most High God." Demons were frightened of Him; they cried out, "do not torment me" (Mk. 5:6,7) and, in fact, were in subjection to Him. When they were commanded to come out of the man, they asked permission of Jesus to go into a herd of swine and He gave them permission (Mk. 5:13). The relationship they had was fully understood by both parties.

We must never forget, however, that God takes spiritual forces seriously. It might be helpful simply to reflect over the history of man to see how many different belief systems have captured his imagination and drawn from him an astounding degree of dedication. Myths and fables have become religions and lifestyles. God not only knows this, He has also tried to inform us through His Word as to the danger of focusing on spiritual forces.

For example, we are warned of the ways in which we can be enslaved. The apostle Paul urged the Christians at Rome to "obey from the heart" (Rom. 6:16-18), implying that man can choose to follow or choose to rebel. James, the half-brother of Jesus, stated simply that "whoever is a friend of the world is the enemy of God" (James 4:4).

God, however, does not leave us unprepared. *He tells us the tactics that Satan uses in His spiritual war against us.* The amazing fact that God knows every strategy that Satan uses (2 Cor. 2:11) is certainly helpful to the Christian who desires to conquer temptation. The apostle Paul says that we are literally in a war (2 Cor. 10:3-5), a war in which Satan not only wants to defeat us, but rather devour us (1 Pet. 5:8).

God has empowered us to be fully prepared for the frontal attacks as well as the subtle distractions from Divine service. We have been given the full spiritual equipment in Eph 6:10-18, equipment that is described as fully capable of empowering us to be victorious. Three times in these verses is this assurance given to the readers.

With all the discussion about the power of demons, we might wonder why God allowed so much freedom for demons during Jesus' lifetime on earth. Perhaps the best explanation is that Jesus used these occurrences in the same way that Jesus used miracles in other areas of life while on earth; to demonstrate His power and majesty over death, demons, nature and sickness. One thing is for certain: it was certainly impressive to those that witnessed what took place.

The demons clearly realized a time of torment was in store for them. The demons once asked Jesus why He was coming to torment them "before their time" (Mt. 8:29). They apparently realized that their torment and confinement could take place before the appointed time (Mt. 8:29; Mk. 5:7; Lk. 8:28). This 'appointed time' of Matthew 8:29 coincides with the end of spiritual gifts. Otherwise, demons would be on earth, and no one would have the power to cope with them (1 Jn. 4:4; 5:18). One consequence of God's allowing these demons to assert themselves was that Jesus and His apostles could demonstrate that they were the representatives of the one true deity. They were demonstrating openly that they were men of God with the message of God. They not only had power over the devil and his angels but also over physical ailments and nature (Mk. 1:22-28; 30-34; Jn. 20:30-31).

One of the chief works of Christ on the earth was to destroy the works of demons, and they realized this (Mk. 1:24; 1 Jn. 3:8). The casting out of demons was one of a number of special signs that were to identify God's messengers in New Testament times (Mt. 10:1,7,8; Mk. 16:17-20; 1 Cor. 13:8-10).

So we come to the final question that is at least addressed to some degree in this chapter. The question is, *"Can Satan or demons possess people today?"* Without digging too deeply into the topic, I believe firmly that the answer is no. To state it more specifically, I believe the Bible teaches that Satan can attack the believer spiritually and tempt him to act in a way that would bring dishonor to God. God allows that to happen. God, however, controls the degree of the temptation and always provides a way out for the Christian to be able to overcome (1 Cor. 10:13). Satan no more comes into the physical and mental body of a believer and forces him to act in any particular way anymore than God comes into a person's body and forces submission to His will. Instead, God informs us of His love and His desire for us to be a part of His Kingdom. Satan's desire is just the opposite. He uses every conniving scheme imaginable to dissuade us from God's service. Think about the following Scriptures:

We learn from the Bible that God can control unclean spirits in the land (Zech. 13:1, 2). He has the ability to control every spirit, including the demonic.

The dragon, Satan, was bound so that he should deceive no longer (Rev. 20:2, 3). Even when given in a highly figurative picture, God portrays Satan as submissive and defeated when facing Divine power.

James tells us that when we sin, it is because we are drawn away (not forced into submission) of our own lust and enticed (Jas. 1:13-15). Our own physical and emotional desires, when left unchecked, will be our undoing.

Even though we are tempted by Satan, James tells us that if we resist the devil, he will flee from us (Jas. 4:7). God, as mentioned before, has also told us that He will assist us in fleeing from Satan by faithfully providing a way of escape. Peter adds that we are able to resist the devil if we are steadfast in the faith (1 Pet. 5:8,9). Another (half) brother of our Lord Jesus relates to us that evil angels were punished and confined (Jude 6).

What does all this mean? Simply stated, Satan can enter the hearts of men and influence them (Jn. 13:27; Lk. 22:3), but only those hearts which voluntarily allow him to do so. Voluntary subjection is not the same as the demonic possession mentioned in the New Testament.

Satan

If demons are difficult to conceptualize, the task will be no simpler with Satan. The concepts regarding Satan are as varied as the religious groups that believe in God. Some believe Satan doesn't exist at all, but rather is the result of some manipulative teaching in order to create belief in an ever-powerful and ever-loving God. The other extreme is represented by those who believe that Satan is an all-powerful being that ultimately controls all events on the earth and could control God Himself if the thought was appealing enough to him. The truth about Satan lies somewhere between these two extreme perspectives.

The Hebrew word which is translated *Satan*, literally means "an adversary." The actual word, *Satan*, appears only in 1 Chronicles, Job and Zechariah. When this particular word is used in the Book of Job, the definite article, *the*, precedes it, perhaps signifying a name for a specific being.

In the New Testament, the terms "Satan" and "the devil" are used synonymously. Matthew uses the terms "the tempter" and "the devil," while recording the words of Jesus speaking to "Satan." In other words, the terms all seem to describe the same being.

The Deeds of Satan

Satan is actually best understood when we read of his activities—and they are plenteous. For example, Job describes Satan in the role of prosecutor (and persecutor) of Job (Job 2:1). In the New Testament, Satan was described as an adversary of Peter (Lk. 22:31-32). Satan tempted Jesus (Mt. 4:3, 5, 10). He is described as one who tries to fool Christians with unique disguises (2 Cor. 11:13-15). John describes Satan symbolically as a "dragon" and "the ancient serpent" (Rev. 12:8, 9; 20:2).

These descriptions are not complimentary, and they certainly point out the adversarial relationship between God and Satan. But though they describe the work of Satan, they do not necessarily describe the origin of Satan. Where did he come from?

The Origin of Satan

Though many believe that Satan is a "fallen angel," one who was in the presence of God and was expelled because of a conflict with God Himself, there are many who disagree. Perhaps it would be best if we could just limit our thoughts to what the Bible mentions. For example, the apostle Paul did not say that Satan was an angel of light, but rather that he disguises himself as an angel of light (2 Cor. 11:13-15). The apostle John in the book of Revelation does not describe the origin of Satan but rather the fact of his defeat when opposed to God.

For our purposes, I would like to suggest that the Bible never really does clearly describe the origin of Satan. Many biblical scholars feel that this conclusion would imply that Satan would be considered a being equal with God. But that need not be so. It is simply true that the Bible never explicitly reveals the origin of Satan.

Here is the dilemma. If Satan was not a good angel who fell, many believe the only logical conclusion is that Satan is an eternal being, like God. In his book, *A Study of Angels*, (Howard Publishing Co, 1994, p. 57), Edward Myers gives an excellent summary. He says, "If we do not accept the fact that Satan was at one time a good angel who, exercising his freedom of will, rebelled against God and fell from his position, then we are pressed into a belief in Dualism. Dualism is the belief that good and evil have both been in existence since eternity, and in conflict with one another, and that sometime in the future the outcome will be known."

The response from the other side maintains that "pasting together" views from various sources may not be the most responsible means of deducing the origin of Satan. Rather, they conclude there are some mysteries in the Bible, the answers of which have not been revealed. In her book, *An Investigation of Angels*, Wynelle Main gives a thoroughly researched and exemplary response to the accusation of dualism when she says, "Many people have gone in search of the origin of Satan. Some believe that both God and Satan have always existed, that they are equal in power, and in ability to influence the universe. Those who reject this theory anxiously seek to uncover the initial source of evil. They seem to think that the absence of this knowledge makes Satan equal with God. There is no biblical answer to the question—"What is the origin of Satan?" There is only one possible answer—"The origin of Satan is not revealed in Scriptures." By failing to establish an origin for Satan we are not endorsing his equality with God.

A fuller discussion of the origin of Satan would be immensely helpful in determining what the Scriptures in fact reveal. This would includes studies of double references of prophetic statements concerning Lucifer, as well as studies of the Jewish traditions regarding Satan (in the Haggadah, which are interpretations of oral law), the use of documents falsely attributed to Biblical characters (Gospel of Bartholomew, The Secrets of Enoch, 2 Enoch, etc.). These are extensive and yet very helpful in realizing how we could pick up traditions and hearsay and pass that along as though it were scriptural.

Certainly, Satan is a powerful spiritual being, but one who is no match for the power of God. In every instance discussed in the Bible, God consistently and overwhelmingly defeats Satan. It is not that Satan narrowly loses to God—it is a total defeat. The power of Satan is limited by God. Satan unquestionably understands his limitations. Yet, he consistently and unexplainably continues to lure man into the realm of evil.

Though we do not know the origin of evil, we do know evil exists. We also know that there will come a time when the wickedness of men, Satan and his angels will receive retribution. God has warned us of Satan's existence, shown us the results of his work, and demonstrated how we can overcome him (Eph. 6:10-20). Equally puzzling is the fact that as humans we are told of the final struggle and yet we continue to give in to the temptations of Satan.

Perhaps the best way of ending this brief introduction is to be reminded of the words of James, "Submit therefore to God. Resist the devil and he will flee from you" (Jas. 4:7).

Chapter 8 · *What You Should Know*...

· the definition of *angel*

· the activities of angels

· possibilities for the origin of demons

· certainties of Biblical teaching regarding demons

· the definition of the word *Satan*

· the activity of Satan.

Dave Phillips

9   THE STUDY OF THE HOLY SPIRIT

Pneumatology

The mere mention of the Holy Spirit can raise the anxiety level of many Christians—which is baffling to many religious people. After all, doesn't the Bible mention the Holy Spirit? And if we are Christians, shouldn't we be interested in the Holy Spirit? The answer, of course, is that we should—and we are interested. But so many ideas, some of which are blatantly false and others which are highly confusing, have resulted in understandable concerns and disagreement for reasonable thinkers. This disagreement has lead to anxious moments that have frequently caused division and alienation.

It is not just the topic that produces anxiety. It is our approach to the study. We do not want to be flippant and make casual comments that are not appropriate, while on the other hand we do not want to miss the clear teaching of Scripture.

Many have gone to an extreme position, talking about nothing but the Holy Spirit. This obsession with one personality of the Godhead, the Holy Spirit, should be just as concerning to the average Christian as the one who focuses on recognizing only "God the Father"—or just simply focusing on "Jesus only" to the exclusion of any other entity. If we believe the teachings of the Bible, there must be recognition of God as he has been revealed in the Scriptures. This recognizes that God the Father, God the Son, and God the Holy Spirit are seen as three distinct personalities in the godhead.

Now, if that concept is confusing, you are not alone. There is so much we would like to know with great certainty. It is here that we need to stop and remind ourselves that we will never know everything about God—but we can know that which has been revealed to us (Deut. 29:29). If you want to have a brief-but-focused study of the Triune nature of God (Trinity), look in the appendix of this book.

But for now, let me try to explain where our study in this chapter will take us. I will assume that you believe in God. I will also assume you believe in Jesus as God's son. That was part of those three important questions asked earlier in this book. Since I assume you also believe the Bible is authoritative (the 3rd question), then I would like to explore what the Bible says about the Holy Spirit. This study is not exhaustive. Many scholars, preachers, believers and others have spent their entire lives exploring the depths of God. But we want to look at specific Scriptures to get a 'snapshot' of what we know the Bible says.

But where to start? Since the Bible mentions the presence of the Spirit in the very first chapter of Genesis (Gen. 1:2), we could begin there. The Spirit is also mentioned in the last chapter of the Bible (Rev. 22:16-17), so we could focus there. But perhaps the best place is a chapter in the book of Acts where Paul is addressing disciples of Christ in the ancient city of Ephesus about their connection with the Holy Spirit.

"And it came about that while Apollos was at Corinth, Paul having passed through the upper country came to Ephesus, and found some disciples, and he said to them, 'Did you receive the Holy Spirit when you believed?' And they said to him, 'No, we have not even heard whether there is a Holy Spirit'" (Acts 19:1, 2). This last phrase is identical to John 7:39 and could perhaps be better translated, "We have not even heard that the Holy Spirit has been given." Certainly, they would have known about the Holy Spirit, but by what happens in this text, it is obvious that they would not have known the means by which the Holy Spirit is given to the Christian.

The importance of this text for our purposes is that we need to know how the Holy Spirit has been given There is tremendous disagreement among believers regarding the Holy Spirit. Let's just look at what the Bible says.

First of all, from studying the Bible we can see that there is a significant difference in the way in which the Holy Spirit worked, works and has worked in the lives of believers. Some call this the 'measures of the Spirit' or 'manifestations of the Holy Spirit.' These are different ways of trying to communicate the fact that the Spirit seems to perform various functions.

Fullness of the Holy Spirit

For example, the apostle John indicates that Jesus Christ had the fullness of the Spirit within Himself. John says, "For He whom God has sent speaks the words of God; for He gives the Spirit without measure" (Jn. 3:34). Others had received some portion of the gift of the Spirit, but Jesus is described here as having a limitless measure given to Him from the Father. He is the only one that is ever described with this boundless gift.

Baptism in the Holy Spirit

The term 'baptism of the Holy Spirit' is also used in the book of Acts, and it refers to something other than 'measure without limit.' Jimmy Jividen has provided a very helpful chart in his book, *Alive in the Spirit* (Nashville: Gospel Advocate, 1970, p. 62) that helps us see the distinction between the various ways in which the Holy Spirit is given. We include this as fig. 9-1.

Several things should be noted as we study baptism in the Spirit. It is never commanded for us to be baptized in the Holy Spirit. Acts 1 records the words of Jesus when he told his apostles that they would be baptized in this way. It was not a command, but rather a promise.

MEASURES OF THE SPIRIT	WHO	HOW	WHY
presence without limit (Jn. 3:34)	Jesus	triune God	He is God
baptism of the Holy Spirit (Acts 2, 10)	apostles/ Cornelius	baptism of the Holy Spirit	confirmation from God
ability to perform miracles (Acts 8:15-17)	selected Christians	laying on of apostles' hands	receive spiritual gifts
baptismal measure (Acts 2:38)	all Christians	by baptism	receive the gift of the Holy Spirit

In addition, it (baptism in the Holy Spirit) only happens twice in the Scriptures. In Acts 2, the Holy Spirit fell upon the Twelve as they were gathered in fulfillment of the promise of Jesus (Acts 1:5, 8) that these men would be endowed with supernatural power so they could reach out to the Jews. This same experience happens again in Acts 10 (Peter retells the story in Acts 11) when the household of Cornelius receives this baptism, which is evidence that the gospel was now being made known to Gentiles. Peter explains to the apostles and brothers (Acts 11:1) what was happening, and he specifically recalls the same event happening approximately 6-10 years earlier when they had received this promise (Acts 11:15).

So, biblically speaking, baptism in the Holy Spirit was promised to certain people and experienced by those people for a specific reason, which is to confirm that the message was from God. We do not receive—nor should we be seeking—baptism in the Holy Spirit with the ability to speak in tongues as they experienced. It was not commanded of them, nor is it commanded of us. There was a group at Corinth who sought to speak in tongues (languages they had not learned) to impress others of their spiritual growth. The apostle Paul spent much time trying to educate them on the need for seeking better ways to serve the Lord by serving the Church (1 Cor. 12-14). We should also be seeking better ways to build the Church.

But we should not overlook the fact that these apostles were given the ability to perform miracles for the purpose of confirming the message they were preaching as coming from God (Mk. 16:20). They had the power to perform miracles, and—as we shall soon see—they had the ability to pass on to others the ability to perform miracles. This is the most powerful filling of the Holy Spirit that has been demonstrated upon mankind.

Ability to Perform Miracles

There are also indications in the Bible of a third category of gifts, which is the gift empowering the recipient to pass on these gifts to other people. 'Measures' or 'manifestations' don't seem to sufficiently describe the distribution of these abilities, but perhaps they will be tolerated for this discussion. In other words, a person would receive a measure of the Spirit that would allow him to perform supernatural works.

Speaking in tongues occurs in Acts 19 when Paul gives this ability to 12 men to "speak in tongues" and "prophesy." It occurs in 2 Timothy 1:6 when Paul notes that Timothy received "a gift of God" by the laying on of Paul's hands. It occurs in 1 Corinthians 1:7 when Paul had been working with the church at Corinth for more than a year.

It happens noticeably in Acts 8 when Simon the magician, a new convert, is severely reprimanded by the apostle Peter because he tries to 'purchase' the ability to pass on gifts. We should note that Simon was converted while listening to the preaching of Philip, one of the seven servants of the church mentioned in Acts 6. Philip was given the ability to perform wonderful signs (Acts 8:6), but it is obvious from this text that he did not have the ability to pass these gifts on to others. It wasn't until Peter and John came that Simon the magician saw the possibility of receiving these gifts through the laying on of hands (Acts 8:18).

So, from this we learn that Simon recognized immediately that Peter had the power to pass on gifts, an ability that was very attractive to the neophyte Christian. Thankfully, when confronted with his own self-serving motivation, Simon the magician quickly changed and asked Peter to pray for him, thus demonstrating a wonderful spirit of contrition. I've always thought this was an outstanding trait—to be able to recognize the error of his ways and then to change as quickly as possible.

We also learn from these events that the apostles had the ability to perform miraculous signs and the ability to pass these gifts on to other individuals. But, the ones upon whom these powers were conferred did not have the power to pass it on to others. So, when the apostles died, the ability to pass the gifts on to others ceased. We wouldn't be expecting people to have those abilities today because of the limits of the occurrences.

'Baptismal Measure'

There is another means by which the Holy Spirit is given to an individual, and that is by what may be termed the baptismal measure. All this means is that when a person is baptized into Christ, as Peter instructed in Acts 2:38, he receives a particular portion of the Holy Spirit. Peter calls it "the gift of the Holy Spirit." As we noticed earlier, when we were looking at Acts 2:38, this was one of the two consequences of being baptized, the other being the forgiveness of sins. So, simply stated, when a penitent sinner is baptized into Jesus Christ for the remission of sins, he receives (a) the forgiveness of sins, and (b) the gift of the Holy Spirit. What does it mean to receive the gift of the Holy Spirit?

By looking at Acts 2 and other passages, we can know that the Holy

Spirit does indeed dwell in the Christian. How do I know? The Bible says that He does. I know the Holy Spirit dwells within the Christian just as I know that God loves me because the Bible tells me so.

What does He do in me? He acts precisely according to the ways in which the Bible says He will act. So, when we look at the following Scriptures, we can know that when someone tells us the Holy Spirit is doing something in his or her life—we know where to go for verification. For example, if someone tells me that God spoke to him specifically and told him where he should live or whom he should marry, I can know that the Bible tells me that God no longer chooses to speak audibly (or inaudibly) to men today. The first few verses of the book of Hebrews tell me that God has historically spoken to man through dreams or visions, but does not do so today. Today God speaks to us through His Son. When we read the words of Jesus in John 14-16, we find that Jesus himself said that the Holy Spirit would speak to the apostles. As you remember from an earlier discussion, the apostle Paul told the church in Ephesus that a mystery was revealed to him and he wrote it down. He said that when the church read what he wrote, they would understand the mystery. We know the will of God by reading his inspired Word. That doesn't mean the Holy Spirit doesn't live within us—but rather that the Holy Spirit is working consistently with the revealed Word, the Scriptures.

What Do We Know About the Holy Spirit?

We do know for certain that the topic of the Holy Spirit needs to be carefully considered in the Church today. If we believe the triune God is made up of God the Father, God the Son, and God the Holy Spirit, shouldn't we spend some time considering the characteristics of the third part of the Trinity?

We should also know that baptism without the knowledge of the Holy Spirit was not the baptism of which Peter was speaking in Acts 2. The baptism of John brought forgiveness of sin (according to Mk. 1:4), but did not bring about the gift of the Holy Spirit of which Peter spoke. It was not the baptism desired by the apostles after Peter was privileged to introduce the practice on that first Day of Pentecost following the resurrection of Jesus.

In Acts 19, the disciples who heard Paul tell of the baptism that brought the presence of the Holy Spirit, they immediately were baptized. If it was important then to know about the Holy Spirit, doesn't it make sense that we need to know about Him today?

A third issue that makes this topic important is the sense of urgency that is created when we realize that God's desire is for all men to be baptized (1 Peter 3:18-22). Once a person is baptized into Christ, he receives the gift of the Holy Spirit. The apostle Paul says the Spirit is then within him and signifies his relationship with God (Rom. 8:1-11). In addition, the Holy Spirit is able to do within the Christian that which he cannot do on his own (Rom. 8:26). But let's stop and take a closer look at just what the Bible does say about the Holy Spirit.

Scriptures Regarding the Holy Spirit

Instead of spending all our time focusing on areas of disagreement regarding the Holy Spirit, perhaps it would be best just to focus on specific Scriptures on the topic and extract important principles.

For example, Jesus made several references to the Holy Spirit in John 14-16. In each case, Jesus used the personal pronoun *he* when referring to the Holy Spirit. For this reason, we know that the Holy Spirit is a personality rather than a non-entity. In other words, we shouldn't refer to the Holy Spirit as "it" as if the Holy Spirit does not have a distinct personality. He is a spiritual being, a spiritual entity, distinct from the Father and the Son.

From Acts 5:3, 4, we also know that the Holy Spirit is a part of the godhead. He is God. When Peter is questioning Ananias and Sapphira for their sinful deception, he asks Ananias why he had lied to the "Holy Spirit" (in verse 3), but then states that he had "lied to God" (verse 4). Peter, of course, is referring to the Holy Spirit when he calls him "God." This seems to be the clearest passage in the New Testament showing the divine nature of the Holy Spirit.

A third Scripture worth observing is Romans 8. In this one chapter we learn that the Holy Spirit (through Christ) sets us free from condemnation that comes through sin (vv. 1, 2). Think of it—no condemnation!

We keep reading in Romans 8:7, learning that when our minds are set on the Spirit, we have life and peace. This brings to mind Paul's statement to the church in Philippians 4:7, in which he says that, when we pray to God, our hearts will be 'guarded' by the peace of God. What a remarkable promise that is—our hearts kept in peace!

As if this were not enough, Paul states that the Spirit of God dwells within us. This statement is made so emphatically that Paul adds, "If anyone does not have the Spirit of Christ, he does not belong to Him" (Rom. 5:9). So I would be very hesitant to say that the Holy Spirit does not live within me. But if the Holy Spirit does live within me, what does He do?

What the Holy Spirit Does

Several Scriptures are helpful here again to see what Jesus said about the work of the Holy Spirit along with statements made by other inspired men.

The word that Jesus used to describe the Holy Spirit to his apostles was the word *paraclete* (Jn. 14:16). There are several synonyms for this word, including comforter, consoler, advocate, intercessor and helper. So we can see that basically *the Holy Spirit is a helper*.

In the same context (Jn. 14:26), Jesus describes the work of the Holy Spirit more specifically as a teacher. He says that *the Holy Spirit would teach* the apostles everything that they would need to know, bringing it to their remembrance.

Later, in the same conversation, Jesus said *that the Holy Spirit would testify*, or bear witness, of Jesus as the Son of God (Jn. 15:26, 27). The reason that He can do this is that He had been with Jesus from the beginning—an additional proof for the Holy Spirit as a part of the godhead.

When the Spirit comes, *He will convict* the world concerning sin (Jn. 16:8). Jesus lists the reasons to the apostles, basically because the world had rejected the coming of the Son of God.

Finally, Jesus tells the apostles that *the Spirit will guide them* (the apostles) into truth and *He will glorify Jesus* as the Son of God (Jn. 16:13, 14). These important functions could not be done while Jesus was on the earth. You can imagine how Jesus intended for these words to be comforting to the apostles as He prepared to leave them.

What Does the Holy Spirit Do for Me?

You may now be asking that if the Holy Spirit was promised to do so much for the apostles, what does He do for me today? Good question.

The apostle Peter notes the work of God the Father, God the Son, and

God the Holy Spirit in 1 Peter 1:1, 2, when he says the Father chooses us, the Son redeems us and the Spirit sanctifies us. In other words, the Father has devised the plan by which man may be redeemed, the Son sacrificially gave His life as the atoning sacrifice for our sins, and the Spirit is the one who sanctifies us or sets us apart for service.

Sanctification, in this context, is that which is done in a spiritual sense. God has set His seal upon us (Eph. 1:13) that we might be His children. We may not feel any different when we are baptized into Christ, but there is something taking place in the 'heavenly realms' that is awesome (in the truest sense of the word) and life-changing. We have been placed in a different category. We are changed from those 'outside of Christ' to those who are 'in Christ.' This is not to be taken for granted.

Secondly, we learn from 1 Corinthians 6:19, 20 that the Holy Spirit takes up residence within us—in our spirits. We are encouraged to live holy lives because our physical bodies become the dwelling place, literally the 'temple' of God. This claim does not mean that God is a physical being living in a physical body because He is not to be confined to a physical body. He is a spiritual being (Jn. 4:24). But Paul makes it very clear that actions in our human body do affect the Holy Spirit. In Ephesians 4, Paul states that our words can 'grieve the Holy Spirit.' So we are to care for our bodies differently because God now lives in us.

Another action of the Holy Spirit is that he is helping us put to death the deeds of the body (Rom. 8:14). You might say, "Now that is what I'm looking for. I'm looking for God to work in my life." I would respond, "That's wonderful!"

But how does the Holy Spirit accomplish this? Briefly, let me mention several ways. First, we recognize that which is right and wrong (re-read chapter 6 if this is confusing). Secondly, we yield to the will of God and obey his commandments regarding salvation (re-read chapter 7 if this is confusing). Then we arm ourselves with spiritual armor that will protect us from the attacks of Satan (Eph. 6:10-20). We recognize that God is in full control of our lives, not allowing us to be tempted above our ability to conquer (1 Cor. 10:13). Regardless, we pray, asking for wisdom from God in full faith that He will answer our prayers (James 1:5-8). While praying, we recognize that the Holy Spirit is interceding for us in ways that we cannot know, interpreting the thoughts of our prayers to God (Rom. 8:26). As we live, we rejoice knowing that God is abundantly working within us to achieve those things that will bring glory and honor to his name (Eph. 3:20).

One of the greatest assurances we have in Scripture is made by Paul when he reminded the church at Corinth of the work of the Godhead. He said:

Now He who establishes us with you in Christ and anointed us is God, who also sealed us and gave us the Spirit in our hearts as a pledge.

2 Corinthians 1:21, 22, NASV

Paul also reminds the church at Rome that the Holy Spirit is deeply involved in our lives. Notice that in Romans 5:5 and Romans 5:13 that it is God who is working in our lives—answering our prayers. But one of the ways that God answers our prayers is through the work of the Holy Spirit. Paul says:

Now may the God of hope fill you with all joy and peace in believing, that you may abound in hope by the power of the Holy Spirit.

Romans 15:13, NASV

Those statements should remind us of the power of God and give assurance and motivation as we live for Him.

How Do I Know the Spirit Is In Me?

I like to use the questions that Harvey Floyd, long-time professor of biblical languages at Lipscomb University, gives us as a guide in his book, *Studies in the Holy Spirit* (20th Century Christian, 2000). They are a good measure of making sure that I am doing all that I am supposed to do as a Christian to live a life pleasing to God. Let me list his questions and expand with comments of my own:

Is my faith in Christ (Gal. 3:2-5)? Many people have faith—but perhaps not faith in Christ. Unfortunately, many have more faith in preachers than they have in Christ. Many trust parents over the words of the Bible. Skeptics and atheists have more faith in themselves and their own powers of reason than they do in the Bible. If I do not have faith in Christ—it is a certainty that I do not have the gift of the Holy Spirit.

Have I been baptized into Christ (Acts 2:38)? The church will not save us—

nor will our good works. The only point of salvation for any of us is found in making contact with the blood of Jesus Christ. If I have not been baptized for the forgiveness of my sins, I have not received the gift of the Holy Spirit.

Am I assured of the love of God (Rom. 5:6-8)? This is perhaps one of the more difficult questions that Floyd poses. But the truth is that we know that God loves us only by reading His Word and believing it. The children's song is true—"Jesus loves me this I know, for the Bible tells me so." The question is not whether the Bible tells me many truths. The real question is whether or not I believe what God has said.

Am I obedient (Acts 5:32)? Peter makes a great statement when he is accused of disobeying the 'strict orders' of the high priest. Peter responds that the Holy Spirit is given to those who obey Him. If that is the case, a very simple question needs to be addressed. Am I obedient? If I am disobedient—according to Peter—it is a certainty that the Holy Spirit is not living within me.

Do I desire to be holy (1 Cor. 6:19, 20)? Paul is speaking of the individual Christian here when he speaks of immorality having spiritual implications. He is addressing their basic motivation for holy living by commanding— not just encouraging—them to glorify God in their bodies. If this is not a motivation for us, then what is coming between God and us?

Do I struggle against sin (Rom. 8:13, 14)? Rather than as a sign of abandonment, the struggle against sin must be viewed as a sign of life. There is a spiritual battle taking place, for all of us, because the Christian is in the constant process of putting to death the deeds of the flesh. If there is no battle, then maybe we have already allowed Satan to take control of our lives.

Am I producing the fruit of the spirit (Gal. 5:22, 23)? The ninefold fruit of the spirit listed here by Paul should be the goal of every Christian. It should be remembered that fruit is always a sign of maturity so we should not expect a new Christian to be producing any part of this important fruit until they have had time to mature.

I often think of a pecan tree we planted in the front of our yard years ago. From the time it was planted, it has always been a pecan tree. But I've been told it takes seven years for a pecan tree to mature and begin to produce pecans. In the first seven years, it is still a pecan tree, but a young one. Our expectations for fruit should be influenced by our knowledge of its maturity.

The church in Corinth had spiritual gifts but it did not have the maturity that allowed them to know how to use those gifts. Paul spent a large portion of his letter to them (1 Cor. 12-14) instructing them as to the 'weightier' and more important aspects of church growth.

Just because we have the gift of the Holy Spirit does not mean that we are mature. We should be striving each day to grow in the Spirit. This growth will be evidenced by the fruit specifically mentioned by the apostle Paul (Gal. 5:22, 23).

Chapter 9 · *What You Should Know...*

- the place of the Spirit in the Trinity
- what is meant by 'baptism in the Holy Spirit'
- four 'measures' of the Spirit
- the difference between 'baptism in Holy Spirit' and 'baptism in Christ'
- what the Holy Spirit does
- what the Holy Spirit does for the Christian
- how you can know the Holy Spirit is within you.

10   THE STUDY OF THE CHURCH—WORSHIP

Ecclesiology

It is almost impossible to accurately capture the beauty of the Lord's church. It is called by many names in the Bible, defined by those that are answering the call of God to be a part of His Kingdom. To conceptualize the sovereign God of the universe desiring to establish a relationship with those that He has created is a mental challenge. When we read the prayer of Jesus in John 17, we understand that it was the desire of Jesus to have those He redeemed to be able to experience the community of God. To say that it is thrilling is a gross understatement!

One of the ways in which the church is described is as a family. If the term is not specifically and repeatedly used, it is certainly implied. We are called brothers and sisters in Christ. We have a Father and Jesus Christ, His Son, is presented as our savior that allows us to be considered by God as sons rather than servants (Rom. 8:15).

At the same time, each part of the church is to consider himself a servant of God. Jesus came to us as the ultimate role model for servant leadership—coming not to be served, but instead, to serve to the extreme by becoming a sacrifice for the ones in need (Mk. 10:45). This church enjoys the dual purpose of being the family of God, with Christ as it's head, and all it's attendant privileges, but at the same time, having a purpose on the earth of living according to the will of God. This will has been effectively and efficiently revealed through the Scriptures.

For the purposes of our study, we want to spend time looking at two parts of the Lord's church. Having discussed how we are instructed to enter the Kingdom of God (soteriology), we now look at the worship of the church (chapter 10) and the work of the church (chapter 11). It may seem as if we are taking so much about the church for granted as we launch into a discussion of worship. But a strong case can be made that the primary work of the church is to recognize and worship God as we have been instructed. So to begin with worship is certainly appropriate.

Unfortunately, there seems to be quite a variety of perspectives on worship. You might think (or be lead to believe) that how we worship really doesn't matter as long as we worship. In fact, many observers of Christianity see no distinction in the way in which people worship. It simply seems to be an individualized expression of people who are showing their respect to God.

Sounds simple enough. But what if God is not so gratuitous? What if God has revealed a different perspective in the Bible?

The Worship of the New Testament Church

It is probably safe to say that one of the most important functions of the church—if not the most important function of the church—is that of gathering to worship God. Worship of God is commanded, anticipated and expected by God Himself. It is the expected act of the created to recognize the power and majesty of the Creator. We find worship described as early as the opening chapters of the book of Genesis.

Cain and Abel both offer sacrifices to God, which is another way of saying they were worshiping God. Cain is told that his offerings are not acceptable, whereas the sacrifices of his brother, Abel, are pleasing to God. While we may wonder what exactly made Cain's offering unacceptable, it should be sufficient to recognize that "By faith, Abel offered to God a better sacrifice than Cain" (Heb. 11:4).

Perhaps you've heard it said, either within a church or in a conversation on the subject, "It doesn't matter what we do when we worship. We're all worshiping the same God regardless of how we worship." But there are serious implications here, because it should be noted from Genesis 4 that Cain and Abel both worshiped the same God—but one was found to be acceptable while the other was not.

Defining Worship

We should begin by understanding what we mean by worship. This discussion has caused many misunderstandings and misinterpretations, which could have been resolved had we just defined terms.

As a matter of fact, there are several words in the Greek language that have all been translated as worship in our New Testament. You do not need to be a Greek or Hebrew scholar to appreciate the differences, but in order to completely understand the distinction in the types of worship, you should be able to recognize the subtle but significant distinctions.

There are several Greek words that are translated as 'worship' in the English Bible. But I want to focus on two of those words, *proskuneo* and *latreuo*, because these two words are used almost primarily in distinguishing between worship as 'our daily service' and worship as 'the church coming together for the purpose of worship,' closely related to our worship services.

You may have heard someone say that everything we do is worship, and they are right—up to a point. One of the words used in the Bible that we translate 'worship' does refer to our every day service. But one of the words deals specifically with the idea of intentional, vertical, collective worship. We need to recognize the distinction that is made in the Scriptures so that we may worship more effectively.

Conceptualizing Worship

Let's begin by stepping back and looking at what is taking place in corporate worship (worship where the entire congregation comes together). Worship implies that someone is worshiping and someone is being worshiped. Easy enough. In the case of Christian worship, the people of God (a term that continually shows itself in the Old and New Testaments) are the ones bowing down and presenting acceptable offerings to the sovereign, divine God. The people of God are submissive and have a contrite spirit. Their desire to honor and revere the God of the universe is expressed through their willingness to submit to His will.

Now that does not mean that people in the Bible were always successful at effectively worshiping God. In fact, there are numerous instances in which the people of God are either rebuked for their negligent worship or instructed in ways they must improve.

We can even find instances in the Bible (Old and New Testaments) that describe different types of worship. By different types, I don't mean different acceptable ways of worshiping, but rather different adjectives used to describe the results of worship. For example, we listen as Jesus discusses and describes vain (empty) and shallow worship when He preaches the Sermon on the Mount. In Matthew 6, He describes people giving to God, people praying to God, and people fasting in order to impress men rather than God. He says that the praise of men will be the only benefit they will gain (Mt. 6:2, 5, 16). At another time, Jesus criticized the Pharisees and scribes because they were teaching their own doctrines as if they came from God (Mt. 15:8, 9).

This, of course, was not original with the people of Jesus' time. Amos and Isaiah are just two of the prophets we read of in the Old Testament who brought the same charge against the people of their day. Their message was not popular, but it did reflect the perspective of God.

Amos describes the inconsistency between the worship of the people and their lifestyles. Their way of living made their worship nothing more than an act that was repugnant to God. Amos says:

I hate, I reject your festivals, nor do I delight in your solemn assemblies. Even though you offer up to Me burnt offerings and your grain offerings, I will not accept them; And I will not even look at the peace offerings of your fatlings. Take away from Me the noise of your songs; I will not even listen to the sound of your harps. But let justice roll down like waters and righteousness like an everflowing stream. Amos 5:21-23

Listen to the words of Isaiah as God speaks through him:

Hear the word of the Lord, you rulers of Sodom; Give ear to the instruction of our God, you people of Gomorrah. What are your multiplied sacrifices to Me?" says the Lord. I have had enough of burnt offerings of rams, and the fat of fed cattle. And I take no pleasure in the blood of bulls, lambs, or goats. When you come to appear before Me, who requires of you this trampling of My courts? Bring your worthless offerings no longer, their incense is an abomination to Me. New moon and Sabbath, the calling of assemblies—I cannot endure iniquity and the solemn assembly. I hate your new moon festivals and your appointed feasts, they have become a burden to Me. I am weary of bearing them. So when you spread out your hands in prayer, I will hide my eyes from you. Yes, even though you multiply your prayers, I will not listen. Your hands are full of bloodshed. Is. 1:10-15

The apostle Paul described another type of worship when he was at the Areopagus in Athens, Greece. The writer of the book of Acts describes the scene and says that Paul looked around at all the idols in the city and was deeply grieved and motivated to address the people. When given the opportunity by philosophers at Mars Hill, he begins by complimenting their dedication to religious practices and subsequently points out that one idol was dedicated to an "unknown God." He then states, "What you worship in ignorance, this I proclaim to you." He began there and preached about Jesus (Acts 17:22-31).

So Paul described a people that worshiped in ignorance. Ignorant worship is going through the motions of worship but not knowing who, why or how one should worship.

This is not new to the first century, either. As discussed earlier, Cain and Abel are described as both worshiping, even worshiping the same God, yet one was acceptable and the other was not. Nadab and Abihu are priests with specific orders on how to worship, yet, they choose to worship in a way foreign to those instructions. They receive the ultimate and immediate penalty by God when fire comes out of heaven to consume them 9Lev. 10:1, 2). Moses then reports the words of God when he says, "By those who come near Me I will be treated as holy, and before all the people I will be honored" (Lev. 10:3).

The Old Testament prophet Ezekiel mentions no less than sixty-two times the phrase from God, "I will be treated as holy." We learn throughout the Bible that God demands and expects God-honoring worship.

Perhaps the words of Jesus may be the most instructive for us. In what may be the most detailed conversation in the entire Bible is an exchange between Jesus and a Samaritan woman at a well outside the city of Sychar (Jn. 4). She has an understanding about worship that differs from Jesus. She would represent the Samaritan manner of worship that finds its origin in the instructions of Jeroboam (Read Deut. 27:4 and 1 Kings 12:25-33 for more background) while Jesus would represent the practice of the Jews.

In her comments about worship, she asks about the proper place of worship. Jesus responds by telling her of true worship. I believe his comments about worship are very instructive, because he describes four aspects of true worship in John 4:21-24.

First, he says that "God is spirit and those who worship…" which is a good place to begin. When we worship God, we must come together to worship. The specific word for worship is the word *proskuneo* which means that we "bow down and kiss toward." Worship is not about our performance for other people or their performing for us. Worship is not a rock concert, choral production, musical production or dramatic recitation. It is all about determining what God desires and diligently complying. We expend ourselves in pleasing God.

Second, Jesus said that "those who worship Him..." which designates the object of our worship. It is not about worshiping spiritual leaders or worshiping His followers, the apostles or disciples. Worship is God-focused. The conclusion we should reach when we complete a worship service is not how great the performers were, but how magnificent and worthy is the God we serve.

Third, Jesus said that "those who worship Him must worship in spirit..." which is another fascinating expectation. What does one mean when he says that he is worshiping in spirit? Is it with his whole spirit? Is it the Spirit of God? New Testament scholar Everett Ferguson concludes this:

> *The nature of God and of the church dictates that the assembly of the church not cater to the fleshly or carnal, the ritual or cultic (Jn. 4:21, 23-24; Phil 3:3; Col. 2:16-23; 1 Pet. 2:5). By the same token, the true worshiper does not seek experiences, emotions, or sentiment for their own sake. That which is spiritual may make one feel good or give a feeling of uplift, but these things are by-products of seeking God and the welfare of fellow believers. Those who seek an individual emotional experience in the assembly place themselves in the camp of the immature Corinthians whom Paul corrected in 1 Corinthians 14 rather than in the camp of Paul himself.*
>
> *Everett Ferguson, The Church of Christ (Grand Rapids: Eerdmans, 1996), 247.*

What we do know is that when we worship, our spirit must be engaged and we must understand we are in the presence of God, which includes His Spirit. We are not participating in a frivolous game designed to attract outsiders by appealing to emotions attractive to them. We are seriously worshiping God in a spiritual rather than carnal attitude with our deep spiritual lives engaged with the Spirit of God.

Finally, in Jesus' conversation with the woman at the well, He says that "those who worship Him must worship in spirit and in truth." This last part, the truth, perhaps means more than just according to His word and will, but I know it certainly includes it. He is making a contrast between the way of worship in former times and the way God intends for us to worship until He comes again. This contrast can be demonstrated in many ways. There is the contrast of the shadow of the coming Messiah and the reality of His coming. Perhaps there is a contrast of the outward, physical means and location of worship in the Old Testament and the inward, spiritual focus of the New Testament. But it would be a mistake to try to read more into this statement than Jesus meant. In considering His words to this woman, perhaps He could be best interpreted as saying that all worship must be based on the truth of God's will and not according the directions or determinations of any man or group of men. The Bible is to be our guide for determining what constitutes acceptable worship to God.

The Drama of Worship

Having stated that it is important not to think of worship as a play or presentation in which we are engaged as an audience, it may seem odd to you that I would suggest that worship itself is a drama. But there is a great difference between a production intended for man and the drama of the worship of God.

There was a man who lived in the early nineteenth century that wrestled with this same dilemma in his own country. His name was Soren Kierkegaard (1813-1855). He was a native of Copenhagen all his life, with a brief span of time spent in Germany. He was a prolific author, and as he made observations on the state of worship in his own time, he commented that the worship had become a performance in which God was prompting the leaders to perform and the congregation had become simple observers. Does this sound familiar?

Kierkegaard was incensed at this practice and said that we were totally confused with our concept of worship. He said that the leaders were the prompters, the congregation made up the actors, and the audience is God.

His conceptualization of worship and my configuration of it may be the best framework for trying to re-conceptualize true worship. God is the Creator of the universe who demands and expects His people to recognize the source of their blessings. He is the object of our worship. He, then, is the audience for our "bowing down and kissing toward."

The leaders are those who are directing our actions in the worship service. The acts are the various ways in which we worship (the singing, praying, giving, etc.).

The actors are the members of the congregation who perform these duties together. When we have someone who is leading us in worship, he is doing just that, leading us as we sing, or as we pray, or as we read His word to determine His will for our lives.

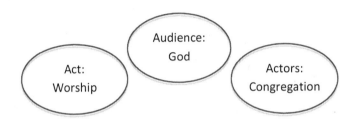

"Acts" God Expects in Worship

Worship is a privilege when we begin to realize the immense number of blessings that God continually pours out upon us. These blessings are not limited to what we can see, but extend to the spiritual realm which for the moment is invisible. These blessings, though unseen, are just as sure as the word of God Himself. So we live our lives with gratitude.

When it comes to worship, what are we supposed to do? Has God explained this?

You can search the New Testament from beginning to end and not find a specific "order of worship" or "template for a worship service." What we do find is evidence that there were worship services (Acts 2:42; 1 Cor. 11 and 14) and that there are common elements in the services that were consistent among the churches. In other words, the order (i.e., song, prayer, then the Lord's supper, etc.) is not found in Scripture, but the form of worship is.

God expects His people to come together to worship in the following ways:

We are to pray (Rom. 12:12; 1 Thess. 5:17). One passage that is helpful in seeing the purpose and diversity in our prayers is 1 Timothy 2:1ff. The apostle Paul uses four different terms that, if nothing else, emphasize the need to be praying for those around us, whether Christians or not. The church doesn't pay others to pray for them or give a certain amount of money in order to have their prayers heard. The church gathers to pray with thankful hearts, mindful of the need for God to bless their efforts in all parts of their lives.

We are to sing (Col. 3:16; Eph. 5:19). As opposed to using external stimulants, the church was instructed to use songs as a means of keeping us filled with the Holy Spirit (Eph. 5:19). These psalms, hymns and spiritual songs were to be sung to one another, to the Lord, and in some manner of speaking, to our own hearts. We are to sing in a way that instructs one another, encouraging us to grow in our faith, and in such a way so as to give thanks to God for his wonderful blessings.

We are to commune together with the Lord's Supper (1 Cor. 11:23ff.; Mt. 26:28). The purpose of the church meeting on the first day of the week was to remember the death, burial and resurrection of Jesus. The divine drama is a weekly proclamation of our belief in Him and our witness to the world that we, as His children, believe the blood of Jesus and subsequent resurrection, ascension and exaltation fulfills the expectations of God for our salvation.

We are to give money to support the work (1 Cor. 16:1,2; 2 Cor. 8,9). Paul continually mentioned the need for God's children to be involved in meeting the needs of people who are in difficult and dire situations. This care and concern was to begin with brothers and sisters in Christ, but not be limited to that group. Paul writes to the churches of Galatia and says, "So then, while we have opportunity, let us do good to all men, and especially to those who are of the household of the faith" (Gal. 6:10). He also instructed Timothy to tell those who were rich to "do good, to be rich in good works, to be generous and ready to share" (1 Tim. 6:18).

We are to proclaim the word of God (2 Tim. 4:1-4; Mt. 28:18-20). Because in the Word of God we have the way to salvation, God has given the Church the particular and specific job of proclaiming the Gospel (good news). James, the half-brother of Jesus, instructed the Jews who believed in Jesus as the Son of God, "in humility receive the word implanted, which is able to save your souls" (Jas. 1:21). The Word of God, when it is fully and faithfully preached, will save the souls of men.

Chapter 10 · *What You Should Know...*

- the definition of worship—two perspectives
- four types of worship described in the Bible
- four aspects of true worship described in Jn. 4:21-24
- the Divine Drama as described by Soren Kierkegaard
- five acts or avenues of worship described in the Bible.

11   THE STUDY OF THE CHURCH—WORK

Ecclesiology

Christianity includes learning about Jesus and becoming a Christian, but living the life of a Christian means so much more. It includes more than just gathering to worship and being very careful so as to worship in a manner acceptable to God.

Christianity involves daily, individual, and collective service. The Bible specifically describes various aspects of the work of the church, but these have been traditionally organized into three categories: evangelism (telling the good news)...edification (building up the church)...and benevolence (expressing deeds of mercy).

Perhaps this classification seems too simplistic for most since living for the Lord includes trying to put into practice every characteristic trait that will best emulate the life of Jesus. Christ is the model—and we should be striving every day to live more like he did. A formidable argument could be made, though, that each of the activities of a Christian could be included in one of these three categories.

The way we live, however, is much more than a matter of mere categories. The apostle Paul emphasized this when he wrote to the church at Ephesus:

This I say therefore, and affirm together with the Lord, that you walk no longer just as the Gentiles also walk, in the futility of their mind, being darkened in their understanding, excluded from the life of God, because of the ignorance that is in them, because of the hardness of their heart; and they, having become callous, have given themselves over to sensuality, for the practice of every kind of impurity with greediness. But you did not learn Christ in this way, if indeed you have heard Him and have been taught in Him, just as truth is in Jesus…

Ephesians 4:17-21, NASV

Did you notice Paul's statement, *"I say therefore, and affirm together with the Lord?"* He was building on what Jesus had already taught, and was applying the teachings of Christ to their situation. Now, Paul could do that because he was an apostle that had received a special ministry by the Lord. Since we do not have apostles alive today with those special gifts, the words that have been preserved down through the generations are very important to us.

You might be asking, "How do we know that Paul was an inspired apostle?" That would be a good question. One reason is that Paul describes his experience with a personal vision from the Lord (Acts 9:1-19; 22:1-21; 26:1-24; Eph. 3:1-10: Gal. 1:11-24). The apostle Peter also confirmed (in 2 Pet. 3:14-16) that Paul's teaching was reflective of the wisdom given to him by God and his writings were to be considered as 'Scripture'—another way of saying that it was regarded as the sacred literature of the church.

In his letter to the church at Ephesus, Paul would continue to instruct the church with specific applications of "Christlike" behavior, indicating that living for the Lord requires a change in daily moral behavior. Perhaps the best reason to read all the Letters (called Epistles in older translations) in the New Testament is to see how Paul would apply the teachings of Christ to specific situations.

This understanding of the role of the Bible is essential if we are to grow spiritually. Every activity that involves man will not be listed in the Bible, but principles can be learned from the Bible that will help us determine whether an activity will build us up or diminish our spiritual growth. The ultimate question for any activity must be whether it is an activity that will glorify God and not give unbelievers a cause for criticizing the Lord's church.

The Work of the Church

Evangelism

- Jesus' ministry was noted for preaching (Mt. 4:23; Mk. 1:14-15; Lk. 4:14-21).
- Great Commission given to disciples (Mt. 28:19; Mk. 16:15-16; Jn. 20:21, 23).

Edification

- Special care given to nurturing and encouraging disciples (Eph. 4:11-16; 2 Pet. 1:1-10).
- Paul describes edification in 1 Corinthians 14.
- Edification is the goal of ministry in the church (2 Cor. 10:8; 13:10; Eph. 4; 11, 12).
- Edification is the goal for every Christian, not just leadership (Eph. 4:16).
- Edification is the goal of personal relations (1 Cor. 10:23-24; Rom. 15:2; 1 Thess. 5:11; Eph. 4:29; 2 Cor. 12:19).

Benevolence

- Jesus' activities were known for his works of mercy (Mt. 11:4-5).
- Jesus was concerned with meeting the physical needs of people (Mt. 25:31-46).
- The early church was known for responding to the physical needs of others (Acts 4:34; 11:29-30).
- Paul mentioned the need for benevolence (Rom. 12:13).
- James emphasized the significance of benevolence (Jas. 1:27; 2:15-16).
- Christians were to be addressed first, but loving service to non-Christians was emphasized (Gal. 6:10; Mt. 5:43-48; 1 Thess. 3:12; Rom. 12:14, 20).

The Equipping of the Church

God never intended for the church to carry out these works without Divine help. Understanding how God helps us is important to appreciating His work in the church.

God has given each of us certain gifts (Eph. 4; Rom. 12; 1 Cor. 12; 1 Pet. 4). A study of these gifts and the impact they have had on the church will help us appreciate how God continues to work in us. Some of these gifts were miraculous while others were not. In addition, some were temporary while others are still distributed to God's people. We need further study on the individual nature of the gifts, but the important point at this time is that God still enables Christians to accomplish the work that is set out for them to accomplish. Notice the following lists found in the writings of Paul and remember that he said each gift comes from God and is distributed by the Spirit according to the will of the Father.

Rom. 12:6-8	Eph. 4:11	1 Cor. 12:8-10
prophecy	apostles	wisdom
service	prophets	knowledge
teaching	evangelists	faith
exhortation	pastors, teachers	healing
giving		miracles
leading		prophecy
showing mercy		discernings
		tongues
		interpretation of tongues

The Organization of the Lord's Church

There is an organizational pattern given in the New Testament for the church. Rather than depend on historical evolution for the way the church is organized, or by following one man or group of men for organization, the Bible has specific guidelines for the way in which it operates.

For example, the head of the church is Jesus Christ (Eph. 1:22, 23). We have already noted that Jesus taught the apostles, and these apostles, through the power of the Holy Spirit, have passed on to the church the expectations of the Lord. Therefore, the Bible becomes the final authority for standards and practice in the church.

The way in which the church is organized is a study in itself. It is a design that should continue until the Lord comes again. By that I mean that the passing of years and styles of secular government should have no impact on the design of the church just as it should have no bearing on the design and function of the family. The Divine intention for the 'government' of the church is not to be an oligarchy, democracy or monarchy. The church recognizes that Christ is the head of the church and the governmental structure is that of sovereignty.

The functions of each role in the local congregation actually lead to what might be termed 'serendipitous benefits' or unanticipated benefits. I suppose, however, if it was divinely intended, it would not be serendipitous. Some of these benefits include the fact that in an autonomous congregation (self-ruled as opposed to being a part of a larger district, synod, or diocese), there would be a greater need for leadership, resulting in leaders that are more connected to the local members of the church than would district leaders would be. A second result would be that individual decision making and participation by the local congregation would be necessary in order for the church to continue to function effectively. Third, there would be a greater expectation of 'grass-root' workers (servants or members of the local congregation) to make sure the joint efforts succeeded. A fourth, but not necessarily final, advantage to the church is a more intimate knowledge of the works of the church by the members of the congregation. With a large organization, there could develop a feeling of a 'detached hierarchy' that is unaware of the plight of the local members of the congregation.

But it should be emphasized that the organization of the church is fully described in the Bible (Eph. 1:22, 23) as recognizing Jesus Christ as its head. With Christ as the head of the church, there is no need for power struggles regarding activities within the congregation. The Bible becomes the authoritative principle for deciding matters of teaching (doctrine). There are, however, ways in which the congregation is to function when dealing with areas that are not specifically addressed by Scripture. In those matters of judgment and matters of serving one another we have several specific designations which we will explore.

Evangelists

In the Bible, various offices (works) are described. These offices describe various roles that a person must fulfill. For example, the apostle Paul speaks of the need for evangelists. The word evangelist simply means one who tells the good news (the word evangelist comes from the Greek word for 'good news').

There are three places that are especially helpful in understanding the work of the evangelist. The first place would be the books Paul wrote to Timothy (1 and 2 Timothy), where the apostle gave him the responsibilities of the evangelist. The two letters are worthy of studying, but 2 Timothy 3:14-4:5 specifically addresses the duties of an evangelist. His primary source of authority is God's Word. He is to study and preach from it. He is to reprove (convince), rebuke (warn), and exhort (comfort) the people to whom he preaches. A solemn charge is given to him (2 Tim. 4:1, 2) to preach the Word with great patience and instruction.

A second source for instruction to the evangelist is Titus. Titus was also a younger preacher who received specific instructions from Paul. Assigned to the island of Crete, Titus is told to "speak and exhort and reprove with all authority. Let no one disregard you" (Tit. 2:15). The writings of Paul to Timothy and Titus are highly instructive on seeing the different ways in which Paul addressed preachers, depending on their personalities. Timothy seems to be a little more timid, and as such, needs more encouragement. Titus seems to be more assertive and needs more restraint emphasized. Both were faithful and both were immensely effective in the work of the Lord.

A third passage that is helpful for the evangelist is Acts 20:18-27, where Paul described his work to the elders at Ephesus. He taught individually and to larger groups, privately and publicly, never failing to teach the "whole purpose of God" (Acts 20:27). That last phrase is very important. We cannot be selective in our teaching and preaching. We must know how all of the Bible works together in order to learn how God would have us to live. "Getting up sermons" is more than just preparing a lesson or two and running around to various groups preaching it. We must learn all that God wants us to do and share that message in its entirety at all times. It is a very difficult task and one that should be fulfilled only by those who understand the serious nature of the work (Jas. 3:1). An evangelist should study to know the entire Word of God--for how can he teach or preach what he does not know?

Elders

There are five English words in the New Testament that describe the office of an elder. In other words, the words *elder*, *bishop*, *shepherd*, *overseer* and *pastor* are synonyms that describe the same office. These men, always spoken of in the New Testament in the plural, represent those spiritually gifted men who lead the congregation. The qualities desired in men that hold these positions are found in two places in the New Testament: 1 Timothy 3:1-7 and Titus 1:5-9. These two passages are given to the evangelists who are going, in their respective cities, to find qualified men to place in the position of an elder.

Two things of note here...First, these are qualities to keep the job as opposed to qualifications to get a job. Second, these lists differ slightly which might indicate a character description rather than a checklist to find qualified men. In other words, both lists are helpful in describing the character traits that make up the kind of men God desires to have in the office of a shepherd. ·

Perhaps the greatest charge ever given to elders (in addition to the comments Paul makes in listing the qualities of character in 1 Tim. 3 and Tit. 1) is in Acts 20:28-32. The responsibility for the overseer is critical because the future of the spiritual welfare of the congregation is at stake.

Deacons

There is another group specifically mentioned in the New Testament, which is a part of God's organizational plan. This group is called *deacons*. Now the word deacon may already sound familiar to you because the word literally means *servant*, which should describe every Christian. But there seems to be a special group of servants in the church that Paul identifies to Timothy because they have specific qualifications given. These are not just ordinary servants of the Lord, but rather individuals to whom a specific task is given and through whom the ministry of the church is to take place.

These qualities are listed in 1 Tim. 3:8-13. Timothy was told to put elders and deacons into place in the church with both groups meeting the character traits that are given to him. It would be well worth our time to list the traits that Paul mentions in 1 Timothy 3:8-13 for those who are serving as special deacons.

Serving Together

The congregation that is made up of baptized believers, each of whom is trying to determine how he or she has been gifted by God and used in His service is an amazing thing to watch. A group of baptized believers must learn how God wants them to work together in various roles. Just because a person has a role that differs from another does not mean that he or she is less of a Christian than anyone else. It simply means the role is different.

A congregation is intended by God to be autonomous—that is, functioning on its own and taking care of the individual needs of the congregation. Elders are to lead the congregation where they work and worship. They are not to try to lead a congregation where they are not present any more than a shepherd could take care of sheep that he does not see. A shepherd lives with the flock and takes care of the daily needs of each sheep. Deacons are working with and under the oversight of the elders where they serve.

Whether we are a member, an evangelist, an elder or a deacon, we are each ultimately responsible to God for our actions. We will each stand individually before God on the final Day of Judgment and give an account for the way in which we served Him. It is in our best interests to serve God by serving each other. When a congregation works and worships together, the result is benefit to the congregation and glory to God.

The Reward of the Church

The reward of the church is experience--to a limited degree--while the earth continues its existence. We receive encouragement to faithfulness, the blessing of opportunities to serve and be served, the privilege of working together toward a common objective, and the benefit of complimentary assistance in those areas in life in which we are weak. In addition, we have prayers offered for fellow Christians in need (as exemplified in Eph. 6:18 and Jas. 5:16). These blessings should not be overlooked or taken for granted. Neither should these blessings from God be perceived only as blessings to be received. In other words, there are times when the church is in need of spiritual blessings and receives them, while at other times it is in the position to be a source of blessing. To continually receive the blessings of God without considering the inherent responsibility to bless others, would be the height of selfishness and, most certainly, would be most uncharacteristic of God's people.

This reward is also to include eternal blessings, the details of which are not fully enumerated, we are told, by inspiration, but are described as being more than sufficient for eternal happiness. The Psalmist states a sentiment so beautifully in Psalm 16, and Peter is so impressed that he quotes him in Acts 2, that "in Him (God) is fullness of joy." I believe if our Creator designed us, He will know how to reward us in such a way that the end result will be complete fulfillment. Until then, we look for ways in which we might serve God by serving one another.

Chapter 11 · *What You Should Know...*

- three words that can be used to describe the work of the church
- how God equips the church to accomplish its goals
- the duties of three specific offices, or works, described in the Bible.

12   THE STUDY OF LAST THINGS

Eschatology

The last topic that will be explored in this book is the consideration of what happens to the soul after death. The English word used to describe the study of last things is eschatology, a derivative of *eschaton*, the Greek word meaning last or final. This includes what happens to the soul of the individual after death as well as the physical circumstances of the earth at the end of time, pre-supposing that one believes in the consummation of the world.

This topic surfaces in our conversations most frequently at the death of a loved one. The family will gather and eventually the conversation will result in statements such as, "Well, he's in a better place now," or "She will no longer suffer any pain." The time of a family's bereavement is hardly the time for a treatise on the state of the dead or a sermon on the necessity of getting one's life in order for the judgment. Though many use the occasion of a funeral as a prime opportunity for evangelism (frequently at the request of the family because of the attendance of certain family members who are indifferent or belligerent toward God), perhaps a better time for a thorough, systematic, and reasonable exploration of possibilities would come at a time when the rational mind is open to serious study of the Scriptures.

For the purposes of our survey of Christianity, I would like to concentrate on two areas: what happens to the soul at death, and what about the message regarding the end of the world in the book of Revelation. Those two areas are admittedly gargantuan topics, both representative of topics that scholars spend their entire lives researching. But my approach will be a much briefer foray into the subject areas, intentionally addressing young Christians or those who have never seriously considered the implications of the study.

It should be noted that I will include special studies at the end of this booklet that will go into more detail on certain aspects of all topics discussed in this book, giving the reader additional material to consider.

Question #1: "What Happens to Our Souls at Death?"

As far as the first question, I suppose it would be fair to say that there are countless theories about what happens to a person after he dies. There are some heavily researched theories along with some based only on emotions and desires. Many simply pluck certain random attractive ideas from the theories given and make it their theory of choice. Others simply toss their hands in despair and concede any certainty on the subject and go on living their lives.

There are several reasons why this topic is important. First, we will all die, and we need to be prepared. Secondly, we will probably all have loved ones who either die or lose loved ones with whom they are very close. We want to be able to help in any way we can, but maybe more importantly, we want to avoid saying something that is hurtful or untrue. So we need to begin thinking seriously about what happens to a person at death.

Truthfully, we know without doubt that the only entity that can handle events after we die is God. The occurrences are absolutely out of our hands. We are no more capable of determining or deciding the location of a person's soul in the future than we have been in the past. So, the simple answer to this dilemma is, the only events we can control are those events that take place while we are alive. Once we die, we are in the hands of God. We can, however, study our Bible and learn as much as has been revealed to us concerning our eternal destiny.

Various Approaches to the Afterlife

In our study, we will see that there are two camps that have much in common and yet differ in specific areas. We will explore two perspectives in this chapter, both having to do with the immediacy of events following a person's death and both claiming a biblical base for their conclusions.

First, is the belief that when a person dies, the soul goes immediately back into the presence of the Lord. It can best be summarized by understanding several basic foundational and Biblical concepts that lead many to believe that we are immediately in the presence of the Lord.

One Perspective

When we die, we leave our physical body behind. We know that there are two parts to a man: the physical aspect and the spiritual aspect. Each is real. Each has a nature all its own. The Bible calls the physical body the 'mortal body' or 'outward body' (Romans 6:12) and the spiritual body is called the 'soul' or 'spirit' (Daniel 7:1-5). We know that when a person dies the soul is separated from the spirit. The Greek word for death is *thanatos*, which means 'separation.' So when a person dies, the soul leaves the physical body. Consider these thoughts:

- Job was reasoning with his friends when he stated that man dies and lies prostrate. Man expires and where is he (Job 14:10)? He knew that the soul, the 'real person' went somewhere.
- Job knew that the physical body was destined to go back to the earth (Gen. 3:19).
- The Bible speaks of the death of Jacob's wife, Rachel, when we read that the "soul was departing (for she died)" (Gen. 35:18).
- Peter speaks of 'putting off of a tabernacle,' which is a word signifying a temporary dwelling place (2 Pet. 1:14, 15).
- Paul speaks to the church at Corinth about our aging bodies eventually dying when he describes a person's death as being "absent from the body" (2 Cor. 5:8).

There are numerous other references to death, but perhaps these are sufficient to make the point.

When we die, we are still conscious and understand events around us. The Bible speaks of the body 'losing animation' when it dies (Jas. 2:26). Of course, James is not addressing the issue of where the spirit goes, he is just stating the obvious. The body has died, not the soul.

Sometimes we use various phrases to soften the shocking blow of saying someone has died. We say, "He has passed away," or "She has gone to her reward." The Bible even uses the metaphor of 'falling asleep' to describe death. Jesus first described his friend, Lazarus, as having fallen asleep. But when the apostles misunderstood, he stated simply, "He is dead" (Jn. 11:14).

Some teach that when a body falls asleep, he doesn't know anything in death. The writer of the book of Ecclesiastes was talking about earthly activities, however, when he says that the body doesn't know anything in death. He continues, "…they (the dead) will no longer have a share in all that is done under the sun" (Eccles. 9:6). This is another way of saying that the dead have no more connections with the activities on earth. It was not a means of saying that the dead go into a sleep, or catatonic state, at death. This is not instructing us about what some call "soul sleeping."

The spirit of the man continues to live even after death. The spirit of a man is that part of him which thinks, and reasons (1 Cor. 2:11). David was speaking of the spirit of the man when he said, "Let your heart live forever" (Ps. 22:26). Peter called our spirit "the hidden person of the heart" (1 Pet. 3:4). Lazarus and the rich man were described as being respectively comforted and tormented (Lk. 16:25). The apostle John wrote that those who die 'in the Lord' (obedient and faithful followers of God) are happy from now on…" (Rev. 14:13). They would have to be conscious in order to be blessed and the tense of the word 'are' emphasizes the ongoing blessing.

When we die we are in an unchangeable condition. The actions that took place prior to our death will determine where we will be for eternity (2 Cor. 5:10; Heb. 5:9; Jn. 5:28, 29). That may sound odd to use the words "where we will be." But it shouldn't sound strange, because the soul lives on after death and continues to exist. Just exactly how and where it exists is the challenge of our study.

In the story of Lazarus and the rich man, the rich man is cast into Hades (the unseen world) into a state of torment—complete with flames (Lk. 16: 24). Lazarus is escorted into a state of comfort in the bosom of Abraham. The two places are separated by a wide gulf which prevents crossing.

This brings up the idea of reward and punishment. The Bible repeatedly speaks of reward and punishment, some of which occur prior to death. For example, we have some rewards or benefits of being 'in the Kingdom' while still alive. We are able to pray to God the Father and have the Holy Spirit help us in our prayers (Rom. 8:28). We have the Holy Spirit living within us (Acts 2:38) when we are born into the Kingdom. We are surrounded by brothers and sisters in Christ who strengthen us (Heb. 10:24, 25). One of the verses of a popular hymn of our time (We're Marching On to Zion) states, "The Hill of Zion yields a thousand sacred sweets before we reach the Heavenly fields..." This is a reminder of the rewards promised to those in the Kingdom prior to death.

Conversely, there are also negative earthly consequences for those who are not in the Kingdom. In addition to the fact that the above mentioned blessings are not realized, there are the additional consequences for those who die outside of the Kingdom. Jesus said that those who are rejected at the judgment will go "into the eternal fire which has been prepared for the devil and his angels" (Mt. 25:41). He is speaking in this context about the soul of the person after death. Regardless of what else we know about the place called hell, it is not where we want to reside.

When we die, we retain our identity. The people who are referenced in the afterlife in the Bible or are described as appearing after their death, all maintained their identity. Moses and Elijah were known in Matthew 17. The rich man and Lazarus still maintained their personality and character. Their respective individual works were still associated with who they were. In fact, if people did not retain their identities, how could a reward (or punishment) be given 'according to their works?'

Someone is bound to wonder if they could ever be happy if they were to go to Heaven and not find a particular loved one there, perhaps a parent, spouse or child. The answer the Bible gives is that those who wanted to go to Heaven made the proper preparation while still alive. Their choice is that which will accompany them for eternity.

The Bible is also reassuring with a statement from the book of Psalms that seems to be so impressive that the apostle Peter quotes it when preaching in Jerusalem on that Day of Pentecost following the crucifixion of Jesus. Peter quotes Psalm 16 when he says, "You will make known to me the path of life; in Your presence is fullness of joy; in Your right hand there are pleasures forever" (Psa. 16:11). If the Lord who created us has promised that we will have fullness of joy, we should probably take His word for it. Our Creator knows what makes us happy and has promised that we will find fullness of joy in His presence.

When we die we will not have reached our final destination or condition. Paul describes our situation to the church at Corinth (2 Cor. 5:1-8), when he says that our physical bodies are only temporary dwelling places and those dwelling places will someday be laid aside. At that time, we will go to be with the Lord.

What is the order of events that will take place? From this perspective, the order would be something like this:

- The soul lives, making decisions on what to believe and how to live, with the certainty of death or the second coming of the Lord constantly in mind.
- There is the death that occurs, the separation of body and spirit.
- At death, it has already been determined whether we will be rewarded or punished. Our lives will be compared with the promises of God, so we actually judge ourselves by the lives we live (Jn. 3:16-18).
- The righteous will go to the Hadean realm (unseen realm) and be with the Lord (2 Cor. 5:1-10). They will be with the Lord (Phil. 1:22, 23). The Lord is in Heaven (1 Pet. 3:21-22). Those who are condemned will go to Hades at Judgment and be tormented (Lk. 16:23). The purpose of the Judgment scene is for God to pronounce judgment upon those who have been unfaithful to Him and to reward those who have been faithful (Mt. 25:31-46). This would help explain why there were protests from those being condemned on the final day (Mt. 7:21-23; 25:44-45). They understood the fact they were condemned, but they were insistent upon pleading their case.
- The end of the world comes at the second coming of Christ. This world and all its elements will be destroyed and God will present a new Heaven and a new Earth (2 Pet. 3:13).

Another Perspective

There is, however, a second view of what happens at death. This view sees the soul as needing a specific place. The principle difference is that this view does not allow for the soul to go immediately into Heaven. Rather, the soul goes to an intermediate state (the Hadean realm—or unseen realm) from which it receives reward and punishment after the Judgment Day.

One of the rationales for this perspective is the need for a single judgment scene in which all the inhabitants of the world stand before the throne of God to receive declaration of punishment or reward (Matthew 25). In addition, the definitions of 'paradise' and 'Hades' also complicate simplistic conclusions. The exact dwelling place of the soul is not identified other than a place prepared for the righteous dead ("paradise" in the Hadean realm). The activities of the soul in paradise are represented by two views. One states that the soul enters a comatose state—a state that will end when awakened for the judgment. Another view holds that the soul is in a conscious state, being comforted by God.

Both positions have similar thoughts of actions determining eternal destinies and God's Word as being the ultimate authority for Judgment. The main difference would be the abiding place of the soul between death and the events at Judgment.

As discussed earlier, the Bible teaches that death (literally defined as 'separation'), means separation of the soul from the body. The body may remain on earth, be consumed by wild beasts, be consumed by oceanic creatures, or be burned to ashes in regrettable fashion. The soul, though, remains untouched and disconnected with the physical body. There was a group of Jews in the Old Testament, called Sadducees, who believed that the soul dies with the body. But the Bible clearly teaches that when the physical body expires, the soul leaves the body (1 Cor. 15:53-54; 2 Cor. 5:1-8). Where does it go? That is the question.

There are numerous references in the Bible that people who once lived, but subsequently died, still had some type of existence. Abraham, Isaac and Jacob were alive because Jesus himself not only said that He was their God but that he was not a God of the dead, but of the living (Mt. 22:32). Moses and Elijah appeared before Jesus, Peter, James and John on the Mount of Transfiguration (Lk. 20:38). Paul even describes a time when his soul was separated from his body as he was caught up to the third heaven (2 Cor. 12:1-3), so to him, the possibility of consciousness outside of the body is not a foreign concept.

Where does the spirit go? This perspective holds that the spirit does not go to heaven, but to a part of the unseen realm (Hades) which is called paradise. Since paradise is the "garden spot" that is a part of "Hades," it is not in heaven. When Jesus died, he is believed to have gone into heaven, because he told Mary not to touch him for he had "not yet ascended to my Father" (Jn. 20:17). This is a critical point in the argument because the location of Jesus' spirit after his resurrection is essential in understanding the place of spirits following death.

Jesus tells a story of the deaths of a rich man and a poor man (Lazarus), each one going away to different destinations. The rich man lifted up his eyes in Hades (the unseen realm) and saw Abraham and Lazarus in the distance. Lazarus was being comforted in the bosom of Abraham, a figurative expression that would certainly have impressed Jewish listeners who greatly respected Abraham. Yet, these descriptions do not specifically name heaven or hell. The rich man found himself in torments, indicating a repulsive and painful circumstance, from which there was no escape (Lk. 16:26). These places sound remarkably similar to heaven and hell, but yet not the same place.

You may be able to see one of the difficulties is our understanding of these words that transcend time and space. We are told by Peter that God measures time differently than we do. He says that with the Lord one day is as a thousand years (2 Pet. 3:8). We also know that after death, our bodies change from a mortal body to an immortal body (1 Cor. 15:53). Subsequently, we struggle over where our bodies will be, how long will they be there, and will we see Christ?

Where will our bodies be? They will be separated from those who will be separated from us through eternity, but not yet consigned to the final destination of heaven or hell.

How long will they be there? Until the judgment day when all humanity for all time will be brought before the divine throne to receive their individualized and appropriate sentences of reward or punishment from God. At that time, the righteous will be welcomed into heaven and the unrighteous will face eternal condemnation (Mt. 25:31-46).

Will we see Jesus? Though shrouded in mystery, this view believes that the soul is either comforted or tormented by God until the day that each person stands before the judgment throne. Jack Lewis offers an excellent perspective that could help us live with this tension stemming from lack of certainty. He says, "If Hades could be conceived of as a state in which the dead have communion with Christ and God, it would relieve the tension between the Hades concept and Paul's statement about departing to be with

Christ" (Jack P. Lewis, "Exegesis of Difficult Passages," Searcy, Arkansas, Resource Publications, 197).

Question #2: What About the End of the World?"

Having answered the first question about what happens to the soul after death, the second question relates to the end of the world as discussed in the Bible, and more specifically, in the book of Revelation.

Before we look at particular verses, we should remember a few things about the books of the Bible. First, each book of the Bible has a specific function and purpose and these books cannot be considered merely as several chapters of a single volume. There are narratives, histories, poetry, letters and prophecy. Each has to be considered on its own merit.

The book of Revelation is no different. It is written in a form unique to the times and is generally unfamiliar to us in the 21st century. Professor Mitchell Reddish states it succinctly:

Apocalyptic literature, then, is revelatory literature; that is, it is literature that claims to reveal cosmic secrets to a human recipient...The purpose of apocalyptic literature was to provide an alternative way of understanding the world, a different worldview. Apocalyptic writings assured their readers that indeed God was ultimately in control of history and the universe, in spite of current appearances. Eventually God would intervene to defeat the wicked and reward the righteous.

> Mitchell G. Reddish, *"Revelation," Smyth & Helwys Bible Commentary* (Smith & Helwys Publishing, Macon, Georgia, 2001) 3.

This means that we should understand that the Revelation was given for the purpose of encouraging frightened and discouraged Christians in the first Century as they were attempting to understand how they could be so persecuted, even when they were faithful to God. There is great danger in trying to read a 21st century interpretation into a first century document. In other words, how could a reader in the first century be comforted by learning that a specific incident would happen in 2000 years to justify all the suffering they were enduring? This is especially applicable in that the apostle John (the author of the Revelation) was instructed to write a letter about events that would soon come to pass (Rev. 1:1, 3).

We need to see the nature of the book of Revelation as figurative rather than literal. It was designed to encourage, and it was written for a specific time. Even though the imagery is highly symbolic, it is intentionally applicable to painting a mental picture of events that would shortly take place.

The general lessons that can be learned from the book of Revelation is that the time is short for evil to prevail, there is a blessing in reading and understanding the message, the judgment of the world is real, and the Lord reigns.

Any attempt to read the book of Daniel (another book written in the apocalyptic genre) or the book of Revelation and make a specific application is highly speculative at best. Rather than reading the book sign by sign, it is best to read it as one would watch a dramatic presentation or movie. The symbols have significance—but more of a general significance than a specific application.

Specific Applications to the End of the World

If one is looking for specific references in the Bible to the end of the world, here is a list of specific references to the events that occur at that time.

Now I say this, brethren, that flesh and blood cannot inherit the kingdom of God; nor does the perishable inherit the imperishable. Behold, I tell you a mystery; we shall not all sleep, but we shall all be changed, in a moment, in the twinkling of an eye, at the last trumpet; for the trumpet will sound, and the dead will be raised imperishable, and we shall be changed. For this perishable must put on the imperishable, and this mortal must put on immortality.

1 Corinthians 15:50-53, NASV

But the present heavens and earth by His word are being reserved for fire, kept for the Day of Judgment and destruction of ungodly men. But do not let this one fact escape your notice, beloved, that with the Lord one day is as a thousand years, and a thousand years as one day. The Lord is not slow about His promise, as some count slowness, but is patient toward you, not wishing for any to perish but for all to come to repentance.

But the day of the Lord will come like a thief, in which the heavens will pass away with a roar and the elements will be destroyed with intense heat, and the earth and its works will be burned up. Since all these things are to be destroyed in this way, what sort of people ought you to be in holy conduct and godliness, looking for and hastening the coming of the day of God, on account of which the heavens will be destroyed by burning, and the elements will melt with intense heat!

But according to His promise we are looking for new heavens and a new earth, in which righteousness dwells.

1 Peter 3:7-13, NASV

And inasmuch as it is appointed for men to die once and after this comes judgment, so Christ also, having been offered once to bear the sins of many, shall appear a second time for salvation without reference to sin, to those who eagerly await Him.

Hebrew 9:27, NASV

Chapter 12 · *What You Should Know...*

- two questions usually associated with our souls at death
- two possibilities for the soul after death
- the events at the end of the world.

13   WALKING THE WALK

The Challenge of Application

We began this journey by learning to "talk the talk" in chapter one. Now we move on to learning to "walk the walk," a lifelong effort in our joyful and fruitful service for God. In this chapter, I hope to take every foundational principle explored in this book and use it in a way to build a springboard for useful service in the Kingdom of God.

I know. The journey in this book has been an extended one. Believe me, it could have been longer. We have touched base with key points along the way in trying to understand what the Bible says about God and our responsibilities in life.

You may have thought that this has been an exercise in futility. I hope not. Our exploration in these areas was admittedly not intended to be exhaustive, and yet it was intended to whet our appetites in wanting to understand God's plan.

Now we come to answer the question, "What's the point of this study?" At least, I hope that is what you are asking, and we are seeking. There should be purpose to our effort.

It shouldn't need reinforcement at this juncture to see that the emphasis of this work has been on the content of the Bible and its application to our lives. We use this as a source to find pertinent information about life on the earth as well as our only insight in the Spiritual realm. This does not mean that the Bible is to be equated with God. God is a living, supernatural, vibrant being. The Bible, as his revealed will, gives us specific instruction on God's will for our lives.

The psalmist said, "Thy word is a lamp to my feet, and a light to my path" (Psalm 119:105). This is a beautiful —even though familiar— expression of the intense desire to know the truth.

This desire for Spiritual growth will be evidenced by our appreciation for great Spiritual needs. These needs will act as guides for charting out a course for appreciable Spiritual growth.

We need an unquenchable desire for God's Word. It's more than just a passing interest, more than an idle curiosity. It is a deep longing for direction. Not just any direction. We intensely desire a trustworthy, knowledgeable accurate bearing in life. We're looking for a clear, specific course for a safe and happy landing. That is why God's Word is treasured.

This highly sought information needs more than just gathering. It needs to be gathered, assimilated, understood and applied.

Now, understanding is critical, but we need to do more than understand; God expects his message to be applied. How do I know? By the repeated stories in the Bible in which Jesus instructs people to refer back to the Scriptures to understand the current dilemma they were facing.

It happens in Matthew 22 when Sadducees are challenging Jesus. Jesus corrects false accusations made against him by simply stating that the Sadducees were confused because they did not know the Scriptures or the power of God.

Jesus corrected a distraught man named Cleopas and his friend traveling on a road from Jerusalem to Emmaus with the same admonition to go back to the Scriptures for direction.

We need an intense desire to obey. Now, this is where so many people struggle. We tend to drift toward extremes. We take the need to obey to the point that we cannot accept anything or anyone short of perfect. This desire to obey the will of God can result in constant frustration and despair if we are not careful.

Here's why.

God, the sovereign God of the universe, is absolutely, totally without sin. He is perfect. He cannot co-exist with sin and therefore is absolutely faultless. We can't imagine anything like that. After all, we constantly have personality conflicts, attitude problems toward our friends and our enemies, and challenges with hateful comments made to us or about us. We are too prone to see the negative aspects of life —whether the faults of others or our own shortcomings. If left unaddressed, we can become so frustrated that we don't see how God could love anyone, much less ourselves.

But that is to misunderstand God.

God is perfect—the composite of all that is good and true and right. He is described as "the Father of mercies and God of all comfort" (2 Cor. 1:3). Can you imagine that God is the ultimate source (Father) of mercy? And the God (ruler) of all comfort? Everything that is good originates with Him!

This all-wise, all-powerful, all-knowing and all-loving God, the One who created us, loves us and has provided a way for us to live that will not only bring us to the point of being more and more like Him, but also being able to express to others the love which we have received from Him. He gives us purpose.

We obey because we want to obey. We obey because we love what God has done for us, and we want to share that same love with others.

We need to grow spiritually. For most of us, we know that growth is important. We fully anticipate that our children should grow, and we would be more than just mildly disappointed if our children did not grow physically, or linguistically, or intellectually. We would be seriously grieved and take advantage of every means possible to help them rapidly develop.

Our desire should be just as intense for spiritual growth. One of the reasons is that the Bible gives us so many examples of God expecting growth. The writer of Hebrews states, "For though by this time you ought to be teachers, you have need again for someone to teach you the elementary principles of the oracles of God..." (Heb. 5:12). Peter says, "Like newborn babes, long for the pure milk of the Word, that by it you may grow in respect to salvation...(1 Pet. 2:2). So, if the Bible is insistent on growth, perhaps the best place we can begin is by looking at the Bible for direction.

Specific Instructions for Spiritual Growth

When the apostle Paul traveled throughout Palestine and the surrounding areas planting and nurturing churches, he left evidence of personal instruction to churches and Christians designed to help them mature in the faith. Several of his instructions are in the form of letters that Paul clearly intended to be circulated around to other churches. For example, the book of Colossians is actually a letter written to the church at Colossae but intended to be passed on to the church at a neighboring city, Laodicea. As stated in the book of Colossians, there was also a letter written to the church at Laodicea, which Paul wanted read at Colossae. These circular letters gave specific instruction to the church in the first century and can be invaluable to those in the 21st century who desire spiritual maturity.

Therefore, the book of Colossians is vital to modern Christians who want to grow in the Lord. Paul lists in this short letter a specific lifestyle—one that would require certain attitudes and actions, while at the same time prohibiting other common activities on the part of the church.

We need to be clothed with a renewed look. In Colossians 3, Paul says that if a person has taken seriously the commitment to live for the Lord, he is to "put off," or cease to practice, certain actions and attitudes. This list includes immorality, impurity, sexual perversion, evil desires, and greed. He then extends the list to include an angry disposition, fits of rage, desire to harm people, hurtful speech or slander, abusive speech or obscene language. They were to quit lying to each other and begin to act like brothers in Christ.

In addition to those things to reject from one's lifestyle, Paul gives the goal for a Christian, which he characterizes as exemplary for those who are chosen of God. They (we) are to "put on," or have, hearts of compassion, kindness, humility, gentleness and patience. We are to be patient and forgiving and do those things that build up love between brothers and sisters in Christ.

These new lives are to be characteristic of our love for God and our commitment to the church, which is the body of Christ. A major life change is appropriate for those who have been made new in Christ. These teachings are consistent with other Scriptures which emphasize the need for the body of Christ to live in peace, harmony and mutual edification (building each other up).

We need to be assured that we are secure in our salvation. Many people have doubts about their spiritual status with the Lord. Have I been saved? Am I not saved? Can I ever reach a point where I can know that I am in a saved relationship with Christ?

While this question is very valuable in bringing someone to the Lord, it can be detrimental if the person who obeys God continually questions his status of salvation. (At this point, it might be helpful to go back over Chapter 7 on soteriology, where the process through which God saves a man is more fully explained). If a person is never convinced that he is saved, he will have little comfort in life and certainly very little comfort to offer to someone else who is seeking a relationship with the Lord.

Fortunately, the intent of God was not to leave us in an eternal quandary. God meant for us to know our spiritual status at any one given point in time. We know this because the Bible continually offers comfort to those who are faithful. This is best demonstrated by the apostle John in the letter we know as 1 John. Notice these key Scriptures in this short book that help us determine whether we are in Christ or not. The first test is found in 1 John 2:3-6 and can best be summarized by answering the question, "Am I obedient to the teachings of God?" The second test is found in 1 John 3:18, best summarized by answering "Do I love my brothers and sisters in Christ (fellow Christians)?" The third test is found in 1 John 5:13, summarized by answering "Do I believe in Jesus?"

These three tests are very helpful in giving comfort to the disciples of Christ. John explicitly states his intentions in this letter when he says, "These things I have written to you who believe in the name of the Son of God, in order that you may know that you have eternal life" (1 Jn. 5:13). John clearly intended to offer comfort and confidence to those who were obedient to the will of God as found in the Scriptures, loved their brothers and sisters in Christ, and believed in Jesus Christ. By answering the same questions in the affirmative today, we can have the same assurance.

We need to accept the challenge of living the Christian life. Being satisfied with one's salvation and falling into a lethargic lifestyle as a Christian was never the intent of our Lord. We now have the privilege and opportunity to live for the Lord on a daily basis in a way that brings glory to God for all that He has done (1 Pet. 2:9). This lifestyle is best identified by opening the Bible and learning about ways in which we can serve.

We need to accept the challenge of living for God each day. Paul wrote to the church at Rome and said that we are to offer our bodies as a living sacrifice (Rom. 12:1, 2). This living sacrifice calls for daily commitments of life and service. This will be the greatest challenge we will ever face. Let's look at specific Scriptures that discuss the challenge.

First, there is the challenge of hearing the call. The apostle Peter discusses this at length in his two letters. (Fuller treatment of these principles from Peter is explored in my book, *Living the Dream*). For our purposes, perhaps it is best just to note the calls under consideration....

- We have been called to live holy lives (1 Pet. 1:14)
- We have been called to suffer just as Christ suffered (1 Pet. 2:21).
- We have been called to be a blessing in the lives of others (1 Pet. 3:9).
- We have been called to live above the world (1 Pet. 5:10).
- We have been called to a life of growth (2 Pet. 1:10).

We need to accept the challenge of finding and using our spiritual gift(s). The apostle Paul unquestioningly stated that we receive gifts from God and are expected to use them in service for Him. In at least three passages in the Bible (Eph. 4, Rom. 12 and 1 Cor. 12), Paul mentions specific gifts given to people in the church. Admittedly, some are miraculous gifts and would apply only to certain individuals in a specific context (apostles, prophets, etc.). Other gifts would soon pass away (1 Cor. 13:8). But there are gifts that are given "to each one individually just as He (the Spirit) wills" (1 Cor. 12:11). It is the task of the Christian to find his gifts and subsequently use them in service to God.

The fact that God gives us gifts should not shock or surprise us. The fact that we sometimes go an entire lifetime without seriously considering what God may have gifted us to do should deeply sadden us. We are given gifts for a reason, which is to use them in service to God.

We need to accept the challenge of acting on what we know. It's not what we do not know about the Bible and God's will that will lead to our own spiritual demise. It is that we don't act on that which we know.

Jesus ended His Sermon on the Mount with the parable of the wise and the foolish builder (Mt. 7: 24-27). The wise man was the one who built his house on a strong foundation of a rock, one that would withstand the storms destined to pass by. The foolish man built his house on a foundation of sand, and was destined to have his entire house washed away in the violent storm. He summarized by saying that the wise man is the one who hears what he should do and acts on it. The foolish man is the one who listens but does not obey. The wise man listens and *acts*.

We need to accept the challenge of walking the walk. Walking the walk is more than just talking the talk (you'll have to excuse the reference to the first chapter in this book). It is recognizing that our spiritual lives are of vital interest to God. He loves us and desires that each of us make daily decisions for Him.

Paul's letter to the church at Ephesus is highly instructive on identifying the walk. In fact, the word "walk," which is best understood as a 'way of life,' is used by Paul five times in the last three chapters of the book. Look at his use of the word and see if it can't help us understand the task of living daily for God.

- We are to walk in a manner worthy of our calling (Eph. 4:1).
- We are to walk in a way distinctly different from that of the world (Eph. 4:17).
- We are to walk in love, indicated by our speech and our actions (Eph. 5:2).
- We are to walk as children of light, trying to learn what pleases God (Eph. 5:8).
- We are to walk carefully, understanding our time is limited (Eph. 5:15).

These are outstanding markers for us with each indicating the goal of our daily walk. When we see we are not heading in the right direction, corrective action on our part is necessary. This corrective action may take the place of confession, prayer, study and fellowship. We must not just talk the talk—we must walk the walk.

We need to accept the challenge of finding joy in service. Perhaps this is our greatest challenge. One passage written by Paul to the church at Philippi may serve as a good reminder for us when it seems that we are pulled in every direction or frustrated by our lack of ability to meet the goals we have for ourselves. Paul says, "If there is any encouragement in Christ, if there is any consolation of love, if there is any fellowship of the Spirit, if any affection and compassion, make my joy complete by being of the same mind, maintaining the same love, united in spirit, intent on one purpose" (Phil. 2:1, 2).

Now the word that is translated "if" could just as well be translated "since," and in this context, should be translated as "since." Paul was not questioning whether encouragement could be found in Christ or in any fellowship of the Spirit. He knew Christ was the source. His encouragement to the church at Philippi was to be reminded of encouragement, consolation, fellowship of the Spirit, affection and compassion of Christ which would motivate them to greater service. Their motivation would result in a more unified approach of service to the Lord, which would bring him great joy.

In order to find full joy in service to God, our focus must be on Christ. In Hebrews 12 we read, "Therefore, since we have so great a cloud of witnesses surrounding us, let us also lay aside every encumbrance, and the sin which so easily entangles us, and let us run with endurance the race that is set before us, fixing our eyes on Jesus, the author and perfecter of faith…" (Heb. 12:1, 2).

Put these two verses together and we find the motivation that will sustain us through the challenges and frustrations of trying to live for the Lord. We are to remember the blessings in Christ, be encouraged by our brothers and sisters in the Lord, but keep focused on Jesus Christ as we make our way through life.

No other source of power will enlighten us and strengthen us as we continue to "walk in the light as He is in the light" (1 Jn. 1:7). No other power is equal to His power. In fact, no other power comes close.

Chapter 13 · *What You Should Know...*

- what the expression "walking the walk" means to the Christian
- how you can experience spiritual growth in your life
- the call of each individual Christian
- the walk that is described by Paul in the book of Ephesians.

Appendix

Special Studies on Relevant topics

EIGHT HISTORICAL RELIGIONS

Historically speaking, there are eight religions that have been identified as representing serious attempts by man to find truth. It might be useful to give a brief description of each to learn more about man's basic beliefs. Since Christianity is the subject of this book, it will not be included in this brief review of historical religions.

Hinduism is one of the oldest religions of mankind, considered by some as the world's oldest religion. It claims approximately 13% of the world's population, and is believed to be the third largest religion in the world. It has no single founder, does not have a unified system of theology, has no agreed-upon system of morality, and has no centralized religious organization. Supposedly dating back to 1500 BCE, it has grown over a period of 4,000 years by bringing together various beliefs and practices from various cultural movements of the subcontinent of India.

Hinduism contains two main features, the recognition of the caste system (class system of the people) and acceptance of the Veda as the most sacred scriptures. The caste system consists of four classes of man, contained in distinct groups. The Brahmins (priest and teachers), Kshatriyas (warriors), Vaishyas (farmers and merchants), and Shudras (laborers) make up the four classes. The Chandalas are the lowest of the shudras and are the 'impure ones,' treated as untouchables because of their gruesome religious practices. The Veda (from Sanskrit, "knowledge") is the scripture of the Aryans, who invaded NW India in 1500 B.C. These are the earliest Hindu sacred writings, principally made up of four canonical collections of hymns, prayers, and formulas for worship services.

Hinduism is a henotheistic religion, or a religion that worships a single deity (god), but does not deny the existence of other deities (gods). The other gods are views as manifestations or aspects of that supreme God. Hindus are historically tolerant of other faiths and beliefs.

Buddhism began about 500 years prior to the birth of Christ and was made up of people in India who were disenchanted with Hinduism. The complexity of the caste system led to a growth in the number of outcasts (those that did not belong to any caste). People were also dreading the series of births, deaths and rebirths taught in Hinduism, so they began turning to other beliefs to satisfy their longing to worship. Included in the alternatives was the worship of animals. Though many different branches (sects) of Hinduism grew, the most successful was Buddhism.

Buddhism does not have a specific founder. Stories began to emerge and be passed down about Siddhartha Gautama (fifth century B.C.), as the founder of the faith.

> *Works devoted to the exposition of philosophical doctrines or religions usually begin with the biography of the founder. Most of these biographies are, however, largely if not wholly mythical. The piety of the average disciples has never failed to make the sages whom they celebrate perform such impossible deeds as are calculated to increase their renown in the eyes of the people, so that often enough within a few years of their death many of these masters are already seen to be transformed into mythical figures.*
>
> *The Buddha was no exception. Archaeological discoveries have proved, beyond a doubt, his historical character, but apart from the legends we know very little about the circumstances of his life.*
>
> *Alexandra David-Neel, Buddhism: Its Doctrines and Its Methods, (New York: St. Martin's Press, 1977, p. 15)*

There are five precepts taught by Buddhism that all Buddhists should follow:

1. Kill no living thing (including insects).
2. Do not steal.
3. Do not commit adultery.
4. Tell no lies.
5. Do not drink intoxicants or take drugs.

There are other precepts that apply only to monks and nuns. These include:

6. Eat moderately and only at the appointed time.
7. Avoid that which excites the senses.
8. Do not wear adornments (including perfume).
9. Do not sleep in luxurious beds.
10. Accept no silver or gold.

Taoism, along with Buddhism and Confucianism, has become one of the three great 'religions' of China. (I use the word 'religion' because even though Confucius encouraged his disciples to avoid 'gods,' he became one of the chief gods that his disciples followed). The founder of Toaism is believed to be Lao-Tse (604-531 BCE). He was a contemporary of Confucius and was searching for a way to end feudal warfare and other conflicts in society. His book, Tao-te-Ching, was the result of his efforts. Many, however, believe that he was a mythical character, used as a means of fostering a belief system.

Tao (pronounced "Dow") can be roughly translated into English as *path*, or the *way*. It is basically indefinable. It has to be experienced. It "*refers to a power which envelops, surrounds, and flows through all things, living and non-living. The Tao regulates natural processes and nourishes balance in the Universe. It embodies the harmony of opposites (i.e. there would be no love without hate, no light without dark, no male without female).*"

Taoism began as a combination of psychology and philosophy and evolved into a religious faith in 440 CE, when it was adopted as a state religion. With the end of the Ch'ing Dynasty in 1911, Taoism lost state support. Later, the prevalence of warlords in China

virtually destroyed the Taoist heritage. Beginning in 1982, with the presence of Deng Xiao-ping, some religious tolerance has been restored.

The Yin Yang Symbol

This is a well known Taoist symbol, representing the balance of opposites in the universe. When they are equally present, all is calm. When one is outweighed by the other, there is confusion and disarray. Astronomical observations record the shadow of the sun for a full year while the swirling shapes inside the symbol give the appearance of change. One tradition states that Yin, (or Ying) the dark side, represents the breath that formed the earth. Yang, the light side, symbolizes the breath that formed the heavens.

The 'yin' and the 'yang' symbolize any two polarized forces in nature – and the Taoist's believe that humans often intervene in nature and upset this balance.

169

Taoism currently has about 20 million followers, and is primarily centered in Taiwan. According to the 1991 census, about 30,000 Taoists lived in North America; 1,720 in Canada. Taoism has had a significant impact on North American culture in areas of *"acupuncture, herbalism, holistic medicine, meditation and martial arts..."*
Taoist concepts, beliefs and practices:

1. Tao is the first-cause of the universe. It is a force that flows through all life.
2. *"The Tao surrounds everyone and therefore everyone must listen to find enlightenment."*
3. Each believer's goal is to harmonize themselves with the Tao.
4. Taoism has provided an alternative to the Confucian tradition in China. The two traditions have coexisted in the country, region, and generally within the same individual.
5. The priesthood views the many gods as manifestations of the one Dao, *"which could not be represented as an image or a particular thing."* The concept of a personified deity is foreign to them, as is the concept of the creation of the universe. Thus, they do not pray as Christians do; there is no God to hear the prayers or to act upon them. They seek answers to life's problems through inner meditation and outer observation.
6. In contrast with the beliefs and practices of the priesthood, most of the laity have *"believed that spirits pervaded nature...The gods in heaven acted like and were treated like the officials in the world of men; worshipping the gods was a kind of rehearsal of attitudes toward secular authorities. On the other hand, the demons and ghosts of hell acted like and were treated like the bullies, outlaws, and threatening strangers in the real world; they were bribed by the people and were ritually arrested by the martial forces of the spirit officials."*
7. Time is cyclical, not linear as in Western thinking.
8. Taoists strongly promote health and vitality.
9. Five main organs and orifices of the body correspond to the five parts of the sky: water, fire, wood, metal and earth.
10. Each person must nurture the *Ch'i* (air, breath) that has been given to them.
11. Development of virtue is one's chief task. The *Three Jewels* to be sought are compassion, moderation and humility.

12. Taoists follow the art of "wu wei," which is to let nature take its course. For example, one should allow a river to flow towards the sea unimpeded; do not erect a dam which would interfere with its natural flow.

13. One should plan in advance and consider carefully each action before making it.

14. A Taoists is kind to other individuals, in part because such an action tends to be reciprocated.

15. Taoists believe that "people are compassionate by nature...left to their own devices [they] will show this compassion without expecting a reward."

Shinto is an ancient Japanese religion, tracing its origins at least back to 500 BCE. Originally *"an amorphous mix of nature worship, fertility cults, divination techniques, hero worship, and shamanism."* It derives its name from the Chinese words *"shin tao"* (*"The Way of the Gods"*).

In the eighth century, the Yamato dynasty ruled over most of Japan and Divine origins were ascribed to the imperial family. Shinto was established as the official religion of Japan, as well as Buddhism. The complete separation of Japanese religion from politics did not occur until just after World War II, when The Emperor was forced to renounce his divinity by the American army.

Unlike most other religions, Shinto has no real founder, no written scriptures, no body of religious law, and only a very loosely-organized priesthood.

There is a creation story connected to the Shinto faith. Kami (generally translated as god or gods, represent the Shinto deities) include one divine couple (Izanagi-no-mikoto and Izanami-no-mikoto) who gave birth to the Japanese islands, and their children became the deities of various clans in Japan. One descendant, Susano, came down from heaven and killed a great evil serpent.

There are no concepts of the gods equivalent to monotheistic religions. Their deities and creative forces are generally seen as sustaining and protecting the people.

Most Japanese follow two religions, Shinto and Buddhism. Shinto does not have a fully developed theology or moral code, other than the code of

Confucianism. All of human life and human nature is sacred because all of humanity is regarded as "Kami's child."

There are four affirmations in Shinto: (1) Tradition and family is the main mechanism to preserve tradition, (2) love of nature is essential because nature is sacred and proximity to nature represents intimacy with the gods, (3) physical cleanliness is paramount, represented by frequent bathing, washing of hands and rinsing out of their mouths, (4) Matsuri, or the worship given to the Kami and ancestral spirits.

Judaism traces its origin to the divine call from God to Abraham. Abraham's positive response to the call resulted in a divine covenant with Abraham and his descendants. There are at least three major religions (Judaism, Christianity and Islam) which trace their roots back to Abraham. Others which trace their spiritual roots back to Abraham include the Baha'i faith, Falashas, Karaits, Mandaeanism, Rastafarians, and the Samaritans.

The book of Genesis describes the events surrounding the lives of the three patriarchs: Abraham, Isaac, and Jacob. Joseph is recognized as a fourth patriarch by Christians, but not by Jews. Moses was the next major leader of the ancient Israelites. He led his people out of captivity in Egypt, and received the Mosaic Law from God. After decades of wandering through wilderness, Joshua led the tribes into the Promised Land, driving out the Canaanites through a series of military battles.

The original tribal organization was converted into a kingdom by Samuel; its first king was Saul. The second king, David, established Jerusalem as the religious and political center. The third king, Solomon built the first temple there.

Division into the Northern kingdom of Israel and the Southern kingdom of Judah occurred shortly after the death of Solomon in 922 BCE. Israel fell to Assyria in 722 BCE; Judah fell to the Babylonians in 587 BCE. The temple was destroyed. Some Jews returned from captivity under the Babylonians and started to restore the temple in 536 BCE. (Orthodox Jews date the Babylonian exile from 422 to 352 BCE). Alexander the Great invaded the area in 332 BCE. From circa 300 to 63 BCE, Greek became the language of commerce, and Greek culture had a major influence on Judaism. In 63 BCE, the Roman Empire took control of Judea and Israel.

The Zionist movement was a response within all Jewish traditions to centuries of Christian persecution. Their initial goal was to create a Jewish homeland in Palestine. The state of Israel was formed on May 18, 1948, on expiry of the British mandate..

There are currently about 18 million Jews throughout the world. They are mainly concentrated in North America (about 7 million) and Israel (about 4.5 million).

Zoroastrianism is a small religion with very few followers, but its importance is much greater than its current numbers might suggest, since their theology has impacted succeeding faiths because of their views on God and Satan, the soul, heaven and hell, a savior, resurrection, and final judgment. This religion was founded by Zarathustra (Zoroaster in Greek; Zarthosht in India and Persia) possibly as early as 6000 BCE. Living in Persia (modern day Iran), legends say that he preached a monotheism in a land which followed an aboriginal polytheistic religion. He was attacked, but because he had support of the king, Zoroastrianism became the state religion of various Persian empires until about the seventh century CE. In 650 CE, Muslim Arabs invaded Persia and a small number of Zoroastrians fled to India, where most are concentrated today. They reside mostly in Yazd, Kernan and Tehran (modern day Iran). **Islam** is viewed by most religious historians as having been founded in 622 CE by Muhammad the Prophet. He lived from about 570 to 632 CE). Muhammad was an Arab camel-drive, trader, and manager of the estate of Khadija, a wealthy widow whom he had married. He claimed to have received a series of revelations, reportedly from the Angel Gabriel, who was announcing a new religion for the pagan Arabian tribes. When he presented his message in Mecca, he was at first ignored and then threatened with death. So he took his wife, his kinsman, Abu Bakr, and his slave, Zaid and fled for his life to Medina, in the western Arabian Peninsula. In Medina, unlike Mecca, he and his new doctrine came to be accepted.

Islam. The name of this religion, Islam, is derived from the Arabic word "salam," which is often interpreted as meaning "peace." However "submission" would be a better translation. A Muslim is a follower of Islam. "Muslim" is an Arabic word that refers to a person who submits themselves to the will of God. Many Muslims are offended by the phrases

"Islamic terrorist" or "Muslim terrorist," which have been observed so often in the media; they are viewed as oxymorons.

Followers of Islam are called **Muslims**. "Allah" is an Arabic word which means "the One True God." An alternative spelling for "Muslim" that is occasionally used is "Moslim"; it is not recommended because it is often pronounced "mawzlem": which sounds like an Arabic word for "oppressor". Some Western writers in the past have referred to Islam as "Mohammedism"; this is deeply offensive to many Muslims, as its usage can lead some to the concept that Muhammad the Prophet was in some way divine.

By 750 CE, Islam had expanded to China, India, along the Southern shore of the Mediterranean and into Spain. By 1550, they had reached Vienna. Wars resulted, expelling Muslims from Spain and Europe. Since their trading routes were mostly over land, they did not develop an extensive sea trade (as, for example, the English and Spaniards). As a result, the old world occupation of North America was left to Christians.

Believers are currently concentrated from the West coast of Africa to the Philippines. In Africa, in particular, they are increasing in numbers, largely at the expense of Christianity.

Many do not look upon Islam as a new religion. They feel that it is, in reality, the faith taught by the ancient Prophets, Abraham, David, Moses and Jesus. Muhammad's role as the last of the Prophets was to formalize and clarify the faith and to purify it by removing foreign ideas that had been added in error.

There are five claims made by Muslims regarding the Qur'an (the transcription of the oracles given to Muhammad). First, Muslims believe it to be, in its entirety, the infallible word of God, since the message is claimed to have been received from Gabriel. Second, it is claimed that the events of Muhammad's life and those of the Arabian peoples have not been mingled with the "divine verses" of the Qur'an, as in the case of the Bible. In other words, every word of the Qur'an is divine and to be considered authoritative. Third, it is claimed that the Arabic language is still in use after 1400 years, thus preserving the original text of the Qur'an with its original meanings. Fourth, it is claimed that the Qur'an was eternally pre-existent. Fifth, Islamic scholars say that the Qur'an is the final revelation of God, superseding all previous revelations.

Who is Muhammad?

(Muhammad is also spelled Mohammed)

While still young, Muhammad (also spelled Mohammed), was sent into the desert to be raised by a foster family. This was common practice at the time. He was orphaned at age 6 and was brought up by his uncle. As a child, he worked as a shepherd. He was taken on a caravan to Syria by his uncle at the age of 9 (or 12). Later, as a youth, he was employed as a camel driver on the trade routes between Syria and Arabia. Muhammad later managed caravans on behalf of merchants. He met people of different religious beliefs on his travels, and was able to observe and learn about Judaism, Christianity and the indigenous pagan religions.

After marriage, he was able to spend more time in meditation. At the age of 40 (610 CE), he claimed to have been visited in Mecca by the angel Gabriel. He developed the conviction that he had been ordained a prophet and given the task of converting his countrymen from their pagan, polytheistic beliefs and what he regarded as moral decadence, idolatry, hedonism and materialism.

He met considerable opposition to his teachings. In 622 CE, due to increasing persecution, he moved north to Medina. The trek is known as the hegira. Here he was disappointed by the rejection of his message by the Jews. Through religious discussion, persuasion, military activity and political negotiation, Muhammad became the most powerful leader in Arabia, and Islam was firmly established throughout the area.

Dave Phillips

DOES WORSHIP REALLY MATTER?

Does God care about all the details?

A common refrain heard from many people is that God doesn't really care about the specific activities that take place in a worship service. After all, isn't God looking at our hearts? Of course, the correct answer is that God is absolutely concerned with the motivation of our hearts as we worship. Some of the most scathing comments made in the Old Testament was about the hearts of the worshipers who seemed so obsessed with the minutiae of worship that they forgot the purpose of worship *(Read Samuel's instructions to King Saul in 1 Samuel 15:20-25, or the prophet Amos's comments regarding worship in Amos 4:4-6 and Amos 5:21-24, or the words of Micah regarding the will of God in Micah 6:6-8).*

It would certainly be a mistake to think that God does not look at the manner of our worship—that is, the specific acts. There are a few examples in the Old Testament that we simply cannot dismiss. We neglect to learn from these events at our own peril.

For example, what about Cain and Abel? Both worshiped the same God—but only one was worshiping in a way that was acceptable to God. You see, it is possible to worship the same God but both not be acceptable. Read Genesis 4 again and see what God was expecting from Cain.

A second story that is difficult to overlook is the sin of Nadab and Abihu (Lev. 10:1-11). These two priests were given specific instructions on the fire that was to be used in burning incense to the Lord, but they were consumed by fire coming down out of heaven because they used "strange fire." Though the specific source of 'strange fire' is not given (strange incense was incense not prepared according to the Divine prescription in Ex. 30:9) the text plainly states that the fire was that "which He had not commanded them."

It seems God does care about details.

And then there is the story of the Israelites moving the Ark of the Covenant in 1 Samuel 6 and 2 Samuel 6. Read both chapters and you'll get a sense of what is transpiring.

In 1 Samuel 6, the Israelites bring the Ark of the Covenant into the battlefield to help them overcome the Philistines. The Philistines, however, conquered the Israelites during the battle and took the ark with them. But, every city where they placed the ark suddenly experienced a plague of tumors and rats. In desperation, they contrived a plan to place the ark on a freshly built cart which would be pulled by two cows that had just given birth to calves. It was a test to see if this would appease the God of Israel. After all, the Philistines didn't worship the God of the Israelites but rather worshiped other gods. They had no idea that God had already designated the manner in which the Ark of the Covenant was to be carried—by pre-attached poles. The Jews undoubtedly knew this. Regardless, the ark finally made its way back to the Israelites to the delight of God's people.

The problem came (as told in 2 Sam. 6) when David decided to bring the Ark of the Covenant back to Jerusalem. When he loaded the ark on a new cart—after all, that is the way it came back into the camp of the Israelites—the cart ran into a ditch, almost upsetting the ark, and the priest who reached out to steady the ark (touching it was prohibited by God), was immediately killed by the Lord. David later explains (1 Chron. 15:13) that the Lord did not receive the respect that He required. When they later attempted to bring the ark back to Jerusalem according to the manner in which they were instructed, everything was fine.

It is difficult to overlook such important lessons.

When we speak of worship, it can be tempting to rationalize and explain those activities that are so enjoyable and so frequently enjoyed by those around us. I mean, why would we want to cause more divisions about matters that don't seem to make that much difference? Don't we have enough division? Aren't we running into obstacle after obstacle in trying to worship acceptably to God?

But then, where will we cease to compromise—if we ever decide to cease compromising? Is there no line at all? Will we accept anything or everything people want to offer as worship?

Is the perspective of God ever seriously considered? Or is it a vote of the majority that becomes our guiding principle? Is it the perception of the impact it will have on non-believers that becomes the deciding factor?

When Paul wrote to the church at Corinth (1 Cor. 14:23), he was concerned about the impact that the worship service would have on unbelievers. His response was not to alter the worship service to accommodate the outsider, but rather explain to the outsider what the believers were doing in worship. He was visitor-conscious but not visitor-driven.

Worship does matter to God. It should also matter to us. For example, there is an excellent illustration of these principles shortly following the time of King Solomon. Read 1 Kings 12:1-33 and notice the drastic changes that take place following Solomon's death. His son, Rehoboam must make a decision regarding the heavy taxation laid upon the nation. When King Rehoboam decides not to lighten the taxes on the people of Israel, Jeroboam decides to institute a civil war that not only succeeds in dividing the people in royal allegiance, but also religious allegiance.

The specific lesson that can be learned from reading of the scheme of Jeroboam is that poor decisions can have disastrous consequences that are passed down from generation to generation, consequences that are not only irreversible, but leave cataclysmic penalties on descendants.

The main points appear quite obviously in the text and are very interesting once we understand the full story of the events surrounding the death of Solomon and the subsequent power struggle that took place between Rehoboam and Jeroboam.

Once Jeroboam successfully led in the rebellion of the 10 northern tribes of Israel, he became intensely fearful of losing control of the people. He knew that he had to keep them separate. In fact, the idea of unity (among the 10 rebellious tribes known as Israel) was keenly in his mind when he introduced the following changes. These changes did not initiate with God nor were they acceptable. They would ultimately lead to not only his defeat, but also his contemptible standing before God. There were 20 kings of Israel, including Jeroboam. Each one of them was described in the Bible as evil "and followed the sins of Jeroboam the son of Nebat, with which he made Israel sin." Quite a tragic legacy.

There were several changes that are unfortunate, but noteworthy.

Change in the kind of worship (1 Kgs. 12:27): Jeroboam decided to change the form of worship from spiritual worship to physical worship. In other words, instead of worshiping God in the temple in Jerusalem, they were now worshiping two golden calves that he would set up at Dan and Bethel, representing the extremities of the borders of the kingdom. This calf worship would almost certainly remind the faithful Israelite about the calf that Aaron set up to the displeasure of God (Ex. 32:19-29).

Change in the place of worship (1 Kgs. 12: 29). Jeroboam knew that God wanted the people to go to the temple in Jerusalem, but he knew that if they worshiped together they would grow closer together—and ultimately leave him and eventually take his life. By insinuating that he was thinking of their needs ("it is too much for you to go up to Jerusalem"), Jeroboam is transparent in his desire to keep them away from the city where Judah would be present. He knew that if they worshiped together, they would eventually be united together in their service to God.

Change in the priests (1 Kgs. 12:31). Jeroboam no longer recognized God's requirement that a priest must be of the priestly tribe of Aaron in order to serve. In what again would be an obvious change from obedience to the divine restrictions for priesthood, Jeroboam would be the one who decided who could become a spiritual leader in the worship of God. The result was that the tribe specifically designated to be priests would abandon the Israelites and return to Judah (2 Chron. 11:14).

Change in the time for worship (1 Kgs. 12:32). In this act, Jeroboam reveals that he recognized the commandment of God regarding the time of worship and knew the significance that the people placed on worship itself. God had commanded the Jews to worship in the seventh month, but he instituted a system of worship for the northern kingdom on the eighth month. It might not have seemed like much of a change, but it was indeed a change.

These places of worship (called high places) were detestable in the sight of God because they did not bring God honor by disobedience to His direct commands.

As is true with most things in life, disobedience doesn't usually occur overnight. There are incremental moves that steadily and progressively take a person further and further away from God. Paul warned the church at Corinth (1 Cor. 10:1-12), the church at Rome (Rom. 1:18-32), and the church at Thessalonica (2 Thess. 2:9-12). We need to learn the lesson today.

A BRIEF STUDY OF THE TRINITY

The study of God is a most challenging and rewarding adventure. We are faced with a serious dilemma. We avoid the subject and risk ignoring one of the most powerful teachings of the New Testament. We obsess about the topic and risk believing every teaching as if it came from God. Many good works have been condemned because of false views of what God can and should be doing. On the other hand, many terrible atrocities in the world have been committed in the name of God, and specifically, of what God "told" people to do in the midst of adversity.

The word "Trinity" doesn't appear in the Bible. The concept is all through the Bible. For example, the Bible repeatedly mentions God the Father, God the Son, and God the Holy Spirit. Each of the three was considered as a unique personality. Yet these distinct personages, or personalities, are completely united in the concept of the one God. This is the concept of the 'Trinity,' or as it has been called, the Triune God.

Now how does this concept of the Trinity work? Briefly, let me give three illustrations commonly used, discuss the limitations of their application, and then try to give a healthy way of understanding the concept.

Many teach that the Godhead (or triune God) is like an apple. There is only one apple. Yet, the apple has three distinct parts—the peeling, the inside of the apple, and the apple core. At first glance it may seem this is appropriate. Three distinct parts with one unified whole. The weakness of the illustration is that the three parts are so distinct that they are not like each other. Jesus said that, "if you have seen me, you have seen the Father (Jn. 14:9). The writer of the book of Hebrews says that Jesus is the exact representation of the Father (Heb. 1:3).

Still others teach that the Godhead is like an egg. Same principle, there is only one egg—with three distinct parts. But this illustration has the same weakness. The yolk will never be 'like' the white. The white part of the egg will never be like the egg shell. The illustration cannot carry the argument.

Still others teach that the Godhead is like water. This is much better in that the same element (water) is represented in three different forms. The water can be in the form of liquid, steam, or ice. Three forms of the same substance. The problem with this argument is that water cannot be two or more of these elements at one time. Water can be frozen into ice or heated into steam, but you cannot have steamy ice, or liquid ice. Water is either in one form or the other.

This argument also eliminates the theory of *modalism*, a belief in which God is the same person—but comes in various 'forms.' A man, for example, can be described as someone who is a father, a son, and a husband. He takes on different roles, or modes, depending on the situation in life. The problem with this is that you are still talking about one individual who is acting out different roles. He is still the same man—which is not like the Trinity. The Bible describes the Trinity as the same entity with three distinct, unique, separated and identifiable personalities.

Perhaps the best way to say it concisely is there are three persons in the Godhead (Trinity): one in essence, while three in personality.

Every illustration breaks down at some point because an illustration is not the real thing. But imagine if you drew three circles with each circle representing a distinct personality. These circles would represent the three personalities of the Godhead mentioned in Scripture—God the Father, God the Son, and God the Holy Spirit. If they were disconnected (like figure 1) they could not represent the biblical picture of God because they are not 'one.' The Bible teaches that the Father sent the Son (Jn. 3:16), which would make them separate entities. Then, Jesus told his apostles that he would have to go so that the comforter (the Holy Spirit) could come (Jn. 16:7).

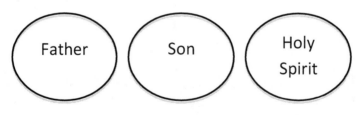

Figure 1

So, they cannot be the three different Gods. That would be tri-theism (an accusation leveled against Christianity, by the way). If they were the same circle—the same entity (as illustrated in fig. 2)—they could not be God because there is no distinction between them.

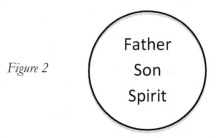

Figure 2

The answer must lie somewhere in the middle. I would suggest that the best way of conceiving God is to think of three circles that overlap at some point in the middle. Each circle would acknowledge a distinct personality. The overlap would suggest that there is an undeniable commonality among them. The three circles would represent the plural nature of God ("Let us make man in our image" Gen. 1:26) as well as the singular unified nature of God ("And God created man in His own image" Gen. 1:27). It would look something like the diagram in figure 3.

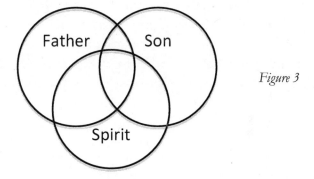

Figure 3

Though we will not fully understand all there is to know about God, including His triune nature, we can know what has been revealed in His Word, which is the subject of our study. We do know that each part of the Godhead has a unique role. Peter identifies three of these roles in the first chapter of 1 Peter. He states that the Father selects or chooses us ("chosen according to the foreknowledge of God the Father..."), the Son redeems us ("that you may obey Jesus Christ and be sprinkled with His blood..."), and the Spirit sanctifies us, or sets us apart ("by the sanctifying work of the Holy Spirit...").

There is so much more that we can learn about God. It is thrilling to read of how God has chosen to work in our lives and on our behalf. The one thing we should take away from this brief excursion on the topic is that God is absolutely united in His ways, consistent in His character, and purposeful in His actions. Truly and thankfully, God never changes (Jas. 1: 17).

ABOUT THE AUTHOR

Dave Phillips is a graduate of Freed-Hardeman University, and has graduate degrees from the University of Arkansas at Little Rock and Harding School of Theology. He received the Doctor of Ministry from Harding School of Theology with a focus on homiletics. He has taught the course *Introduction to Christianity* as an adjunct faculty member for Freed-Hardeman University in the graduate education program on the Memphis, Tennessee campus since 2005. The experiences in the classroom have helped define and refine the approach that is used in this text to introduce a closer study of the Bible to those coming from a variety of religious backgrounds. He has been married to his wife Ann since 1978 and has been the preacher at the Germantown church of Christ in Germantown, Tennessee since 1992. Dave and Ann have two grown children, who have each married marvelously, and two grandchildren.